THE BUFFALO HIDE TIPI OF THE SIOUX

Larry Belitz

Larry Belitz

Edited by Mark Belitz

Buffalo Hide Tipi of the Sioux
Copyright © 2006 by
Larry Belitz

ALL RIGHTS RESERVED

This work may not be used in any form,
or reproduced by any means,
in whole or in part,
without written permission
from the publisher.

ISBN: 1-57579-388-5

Library of Congress Control Number: 2006931316

To contact the author write:
Larry Belitz
12747 Oak Road
Hot Springs, SD 57747

Printed in the United States of America

PINE HILL PRESS
4000 West 57th Street
Sioux Falls, SD 57106

PREFACE

In 1973 I published my book *Step-by-Step, Brain Tanning the Sioux Way*. In the same year, the rendezvous became a national craze. Those involved called themselves buckskinners or Indian hobbyists. They eagerly sought brain-tanned hides for their outfits and began learning about tipis. Museum staffers observed this keen interest in Plains Indian life, resulting in museum directors contacting me about replicating buffalo tipis for exhibits. I needed more information about constructing tipis before beginning their orders. I met with Reginald Laubin, who had recently completed a book about tipis called *The Indian Tipi*. I asked Reginald about information he acquired regarding the making of a hide tipi. He replied that his research had been on the canvas tipi of the reservation years. He encouraged me to study old buffalo hide tipis and be the first in more than a century to construct a buffalo hide tipi.

In my needed search to learn how tipis were made, I examined hide covers in the United States and Canada. My research to see and handle old tipis was difficult since few hide lodges existed. During the 1930s, numerous hide tipis were discarded. By then many hide covers were over 60 years old were falling apart. Eventually I was able to locate and examine a dozen tipis made of buffalo hide before 1877 and a half dozen made at the turn of the century of cattle, caribou or elk hides. I also studied many fragmented sections of lodges. Through hands-on research and my understanding gained from constructing over 40 hide tipis, I learned the secrets about buffalo hide tipis. I found these discoveries important enough to share in this book.

Today there continue to be numerous rendezvous enthusiasts, hobbyists and historians who are fascinated with the Native American way of life. For those interested in the Old West, I was able to document this book with numerous historic photographs to tell the story of the buffalo hide tipi.

I was adopted over 40 years ago by the Bear Robe family. They trace their lineage to Chief Big Foot, who was killed at Wounded Knee. In this book I wish to honor my long-departed sister, Flossie, and her husband, John. They lived the long-ago Lakota values of bravery, fortitude, wisdom and generosity. They passed on to me much knowledge of the early days of the Lakota. Pilamaya (Thanks).

TABLE OF CONTENTS

Tipi Legend 3
Preparing a Buffalo Hide 4
Sewing the Tipi Cover 15
Lacing Pins 22
Decorations on a Tipi 24
Ground Pegs 29
Tipi Poles 32
Erecting the Hide Tipi 35
The Buffalo Hide Liner 53
Unique Tipis 56
Living in a Hide Tipi 61
Children 67
Womanhood 69
Tipi Etiquette 69
Exiting the Tipi 75
Winktes 75
The Crossing of Streams 76
Discarding of Old Tipi Covers 78
Interview with Mrs. Red Warbonnet Regarding Tipis 79
In Retrospect 86

Diagrams
Two-Wife Tipi 34
The Pole Order 40
Tipi Sides 73

Buffalo Hide Tipi

A buffalo hide tipi embellished with porcupine quillwork

Buffalo Hide tipi

The inside of a buffalo hide tipi.

TIPI LEGEND

The Sioux Nation is composed of three divisions and dialects. The eastern group, called Dakota or Sisseton, were the first Sioux to be encountered by settlers moving westward. They gave the name to the state of South Dakota. In the middle part of the state are the Nakota or Yankton. The Sioux living on the western side of South Dakota are the Lakota or Teton. Each of these groups called its living place "tipi." (An "i" in the Sioux language has a long "e" sound. The old spellings of "tepee" or "teepee" attempted to give an English pronunciation to the word that is now spelled the Sioux way.) Each of the Dakota, Nakota and Lakota has smaller subdivisions. The Oglala is one of seven subgroups (tiyospaye) of the Lakota. The Oglala are famous because of great warriors such as Crazy Horse and Red Cloud. This book will emphasize the Oglala Sioux because I was adopted and trained by elders of this band.

Before entering the Dakotas, the Sioux principally resided in Minnesota. Their typical dwelling was a wigwam consisting of poles covered with bark. Their legend explains the beginning of the hide-covered tipi: One day, it is said, a child took a cottonwood leaf and curled it to fashion a miniature wigwam. The shape of the leaf resembled a half circle. This model led to the inspiration that hides could be sewn together as a large half circle to be placed around poles, thereby creating a movable living place called a "tipi."

Preparing a Buffalo Hide

Before their placement upon reservations, Native Americans skinned out buffalo, moose, deer and elk hides differently on the front legs than they do today.

An early description of butchering buffalo comes from Rufus B. Sage in the 1840's. He learned his skinning technique from the Plains Indians and described their method, which he encouraged other skinners to adopt:

> He would commence at the head on the under-jaw and would run a straight line from the brisket to the root of the tail. Next the foot, running a straight line to the tail. After ripping both, he would commence at the hoof and run over the knee, coming out a little below the brisket. In ripping in this manner, the hide was uniform to stretch, although a great many skinners would rip straight down the foreleg on the inside and the same with the hind leg, but this way would leave a gap and the first way did not do so.[1]

The tipi has two dried buffalo hides resting against it. This allows them to remain dry and out of the way. A fresh hide is staked out at the foreground of this picture. (SDSHS, Morrow)

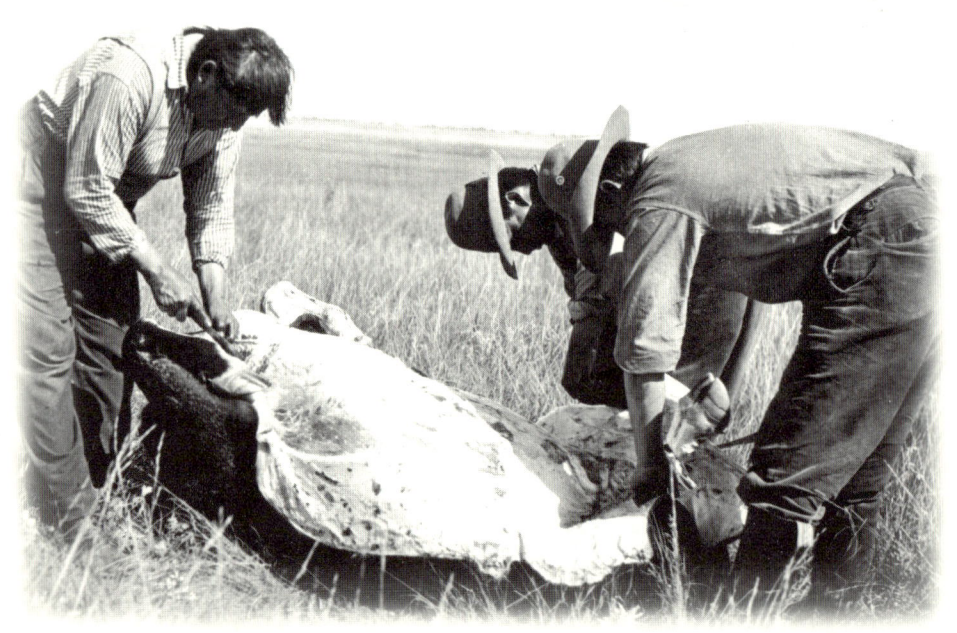

The men to the right are skinning the back legs of a buffalo. The man at the left is skinning along the outside (rather than the inside) of the front leg, through the center of the knee and is cutting toward the hoof. (SHSND 0086-1359)

Preparing a Buffalo Hide

A woman is pounding stakes around the edge of a hide to ready it for fleshing. (SHSND 0270-107)

Once the hide was removed from the buffalo, it was soon stretched before it spoiled or surface-dried. Commonly, the buffalo skin was stretched several inches off the ground with ash stakes. The stakes were placed about every eight inches at a slant to retain the full shape of the hide.

A woman would then start to clean the buffalo hide by using a fleshing tool fashioned from a buffalo's lower leg bone with teeth notched along the bottom edge. A buckskin loop over the wrist allowed a firm grip so a woman could effectively strike glancing blows to remove the meat and fat. In later years sections of gun barrels were used for the same purpose where their greater weight facilitated faster progress in fleshing the hides.

The flesh side of a hide usually dried in a day. An elkhorn scraper, with a blade inserted and lashed to the elbow part, was then used to thin the hide. The hip, backbone and neck areas of the buffalo hide are thick and have a tight grain. Thinning allowed those areas to readily flex, resulting in a softer hide. The hide scrapings were saved for later use as a thickening for buffalo berry or chokecherry sauces or boiled many hours to become hide glue.

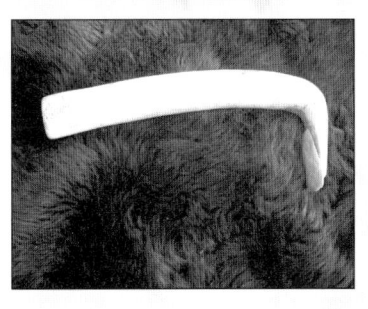

ELKHORN SCRAPER
This elkhorn scraper is pictured without lashing to show where the flint blade is placed. A scraper such as this was used to flesh a fresh hide and to remove hair from a dry hide.

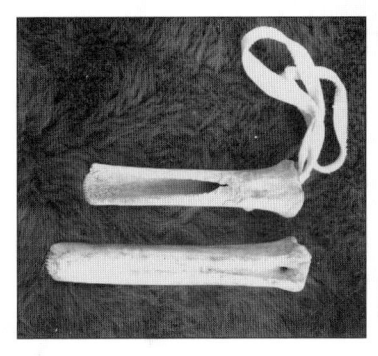

FLESHERS
Some fleshers were made from the leg bone of a buffalo.

Preparing a Buffalo Hide

A woman is removing fat and meat from a hide using a flesher supported to her wrist by a strap. (SHSND 0086-0173)

A woman is thinning the flesh side of a dried hide with an elkhorn scraper. (SHSND 0270-139)

Preparing a Buffalo Hide

The hair (technically wool) was removed after the hide was thoroughly dry and stiff. In scraping off the wool, the upper layer of skin was automatically removed. This would later aid in the absorption of the brain solution.

Next, the hide would be wetted to relax it back to its original size. Sinew was used to sew shut skinning holes as well as to attach the foreleg piece to the neck flap. The sewing would be on the inner surface (or

An elkhorn scraper is used by Weasel Woman to remove hair from a hide. (SHSND 0039-0057)

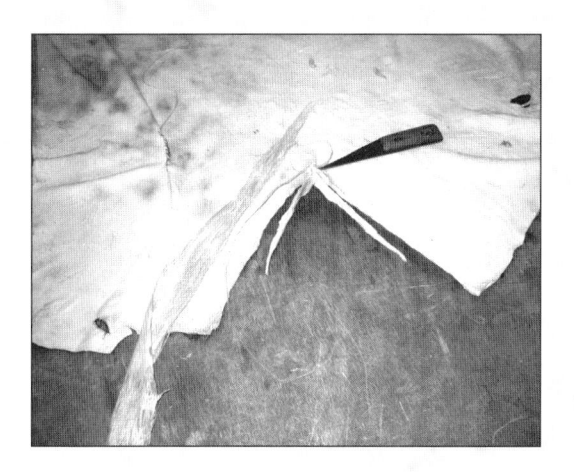

SEWING
The neck and shoulder piece have been trimmed straight, leaving two remnant pieces intact. An awl is used to poke holes for the sinew sewing.

flesh side). A bone or metal awl was used to poke holes in the hide, and the tapered end of a sinew thread was pushed through them. The sewing technique used was a whip stitch. During the sewing of the leg piece to the neck flap, the two trimmed leather pieces would be free to dangle on the exterior side of the hide.

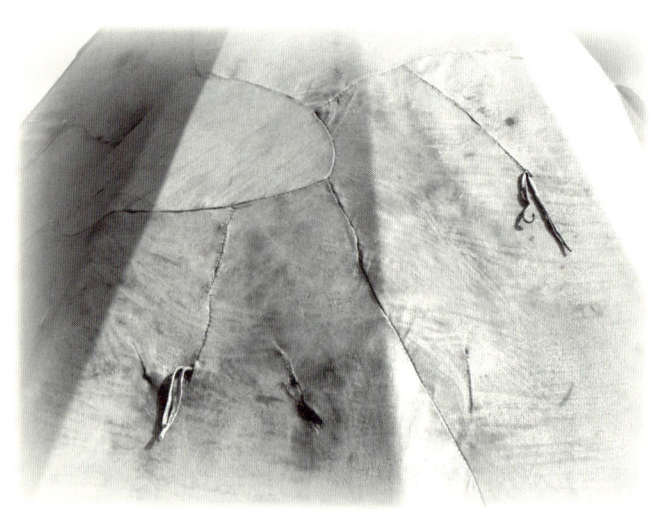

The tassels reveal the direction of each hide in this tipi cover by showing the location of the sewn front legs. Many tribes allowed the swallowtails from each front leg to decorate their tipi covers.

After the hide became pliable by wetting, raw or cooked brains of the buffalo were rubbed onto the inner and outer surfaces of the buffalo hide. Additionally, applications were spread onto the hide over intervals of several hours. The hide was then folded and covered overnight to fully absorb the brain solution.

A key to producing a soft, supple hide was to keep the fibers of the hide stretched while water evaporated from the skin. If the hide was worked by pulling and rubbing until the hide was totally dry, the fibers would remain separated, resulting in a soft hide. If, however, the fibers locked together due to poor absorption of the brains or were not pulled vigorously enough, the hide would become semi-stiff. Such a hide was rewetted to relax it and again stretched by pulling until dry and soft.

Early travelers such as Lewis and Clark's Corps of Discovery and later Maximilian and Bodmer observed tanning but failed to record more than sketchy details. George Catlin, in a visit to Montana about 1834, outlined the steps involved. He described an

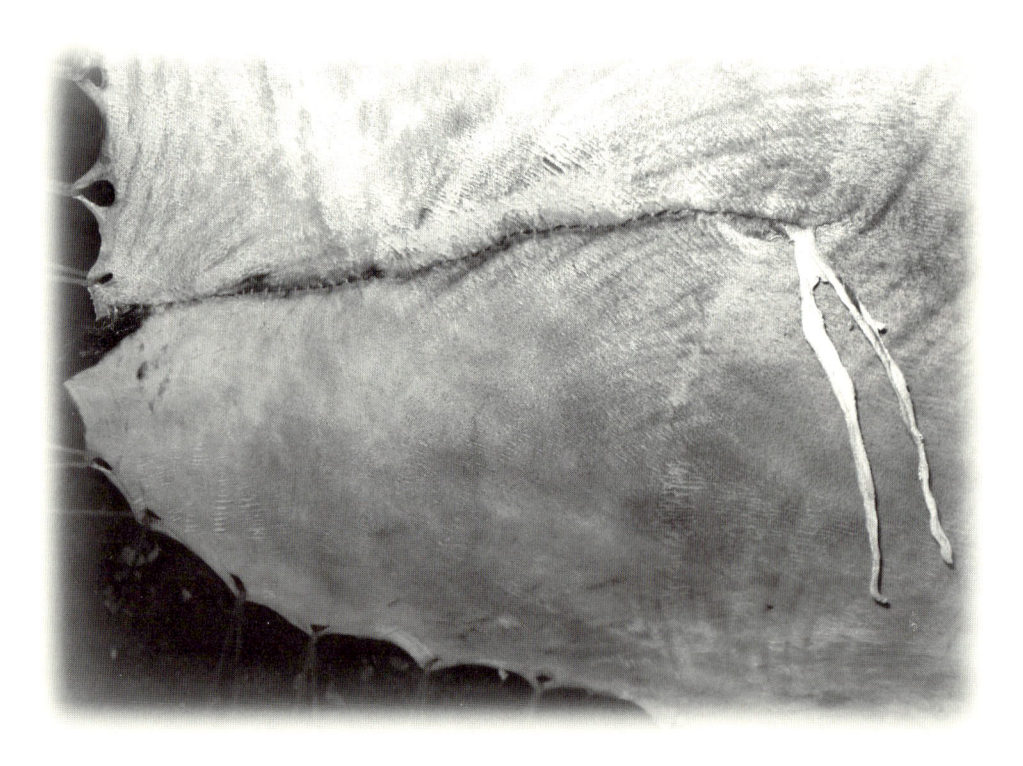

The neck and shoulder flap are sewn and the trimmed pieces remain as a swallowtail tassel.

Weasel Woman is pulling a hide through a twine to soften it. (SHSND 0039-0053)

earlier method using lye in wet wood ashes to loosen the hair. This didn't require scraping the wool from the hide. Catlin explained the tanning steps which he observed:

> First they immersed the buffalo hide in a mixture of ashes and water for a few days that loosened away the hair; next they pinned the skin taut to the ground, with tapering stakes through the edges, and shampooed the skin with handfuls of the brains of buffalo. The women then dried and thinned the skin by graining it with a sharpened bone, usually the shoulder blade of the buffalo. There was a final process of smoking the skins that gave them the quality of drying soft and pliant whenever rain fell upon them.[2]

The most thorough description of the day-by-day process of tanning large hides came after the reservations had been established. James Mooney presented a detailed account describing the tanning of steer hides to prepare a Cheyenne hide tipi for the 1904 World's Fair. His field notes are in unique shorthand that recorded the daily effort and problems encountered in tanning the tipi hides. His daily observations in tanning the hides are as follows:

Three women are working at various stages of tanning. One woman is pulling a hide across a rope to soften it while others are scraping hides. (SDSHS)

Tuesday, April 28 — Killed 27—got hides, brains, packed in ice same night.

Wednesday, 29 — arrived in camp and the hides unwrapped and fleshed and stretched to dry on poles. The soft brains were left on ice. 4 women worked until 8:15 on the hides. Some hides not worked on were unwrapped and wetted with 1 bucket of water each and again wrapped up.

Thursday, 30 — All the women (6) worked together fleshing hides, taking each hide in turn to finish.

Friday, May 1 — Fleshed 5 hides by six women beginning about 8 A.M. when the dew was off the ground and finished at 4 P.M.

Saturday, May 2 — Two women worked seven hours on the hides to clean the hides and later six women worked to flesh some to complete 11 new hides. The first hides have dried 2½ days and they are now turned to the hair side to dry in the sun and are then adzed to remove the hair.

Sunday, May 3 — Ten women work beginning at noon to flesh more hides.

This village has had a successful hunt as evidenced by the amount of jerked meat and the number of staked hides. (SHSND 0087-103)

Tuesday, May 5 — Two women cooked brains and added pounded soapweed. This was well kneaded using the soapweed root to rub the mixture onto the hide. Sometimes liver is added and a little salt. The brain mixture can be cooked and covered with grease to harden to store in tripe bags in the winter. Four women worked on one hide and three on another to do the first scraping of hair. They say steer hides are thicker and harder to work than the cow hides, but they are more durable. Cold weather stiffens skins and makes it harder to dress a hide.

Saturday, May 9 — Seven women scraped 6 hides for the first time and then gave second scraping. If they are folded the scraper would cut at the wrinkles. The work started late because of rain. There are still 10 hides unscraped of hair. These were rolled up with the hair side out and put on a low platform and covered with an old tipi canvas and these bundles were tied at each end.

Two buffalo rawhides are leaning against the small tipi by the man. In the background are rawhides held against poles by a rope. (SHSND A2261)

Preparing a Buffalo Hide

Sunday, May 10 — It rained very hard. 10 hides are out under canvas.

Monday, May 11 — Eight women worked, but the ground is wet. They began late and gave the first scraping to eight hides and gave three their second scraping with 4 women on each. On the first or second scraping they "make a kind of bed" for the hides by putting them upon a canvas next to the ground to keep skins clean and break the force of blows to prevent tearing. Next a canvas shade was put up. Mrs. Red Eye, an old woman, brained 6 hides that had been scraped on Saturday and Monday.

Tuesday, May 12 — Eight women gave the first hair scraping to 3 more hides using a canvas bed under each. They went right on to give the second scraping to 4 more of this lot. On quitting they rolled up all the hides and stretched them. They left 10 still out on a platform. An old woman brained 4. Rain again interfered. Now they have finished the first scraping of 17 hides and left 10 under a canvas. They then began the second scraping on two more.

Wednesday, May 13 — The second scraping for 7 hides has been done. Red Eye brained all 7 alone. 10 women gave the first scraping of hair to 10 that were piled on the platform. They worked all day. There was no rain. The first scraping is easier than the second scraping.

A metal insert from the blinder of a harness bridle is used to soften this hide. (SHSND 0086-0058)

This hide is grained by Weasel Woman using a knee bone to raise the nap. (SHSND 0039-0052)

Thursday, May 14—It rained nearly all day. The women started in the evening to give the second scraping to two, but were stopped by the rain so they rolled them up again on the platform with the others.

Friday, May 15 — The second scraping was given to 5 hides. There was no rain. Red Eye brained these same 5 hides in the evening.

Saturday, May 16 — It rained part of the day. The second scraping to 5 other hides was accomplished. Red Eye brained them in the evening. They were folded up like parfleche and put into the storehouse. Every morning those brained were opened out on the grass all day to sun.

Sunday, May 17 — No rain. Opened up the whole lot of the 27 hides to sun on grass all day. Mrs. B and Wolf Woman put 2 to soak in a tub of hot water overnight to be ready to dress [tan] these the next day. They put a rock over it to weigh it down. They unfolded the hides and put them in like clothes. Hides should soak all night which is the old way and then not worked in water. They used to not have tubs and used to soak them by throwing hot water into the open hide with dry grass to retain the water and then twisting them up with sticks so as to keep water in and then leave them to soak all night. Mrs. B says tubs are better.

Monday, May 18 — They soaked 5 half a day in tubs, one to each tub. Two women worked on each at intervals through ½ a day. They can tell by feel when the hides are soaked through. They took out the hides at noon and twisted the water out by hanging on a frame and twisted them with a stick. They tied them next on a frame and scraped with a scraping hoe [elkhorn scraper]. Two women worked together about 2 or 3 hours on each. They must keep at work until the hide is dry. Sometimes one relieves the other by taking turns. The hide is turned to work the same method on both sides and then this is followed by rubbing with a graining bone to give a roughened surface and to remove any projecting fibers. After this they sew up any holes. They tried to work them over a rope, but then only 3 of them worked good and they quit. Usually 2 women work together on a hide.[3]

The diary continued describing the days of tanning until all the hides were rubbed soft over a narrow rope or a scythe blade. Many times the hides would dry stiff and need to be reworked after applying more of the brain mixture. By June 5, twenty hides were ready to be assembled into a skin tipi. It required over a month to complete the tanning of the tipi hides.

A large hide is being softened on a frame by keeping the fibers stretched. (SDSHS, Morrow 3700)

A woman is pulling a hide across a scythe blade to soften it. (SHSND 0086-0060)

SEWING THE TIPI COVER

"How many buffalo hides does it take to make a tipi?" is a frequent question. The answer is based on the assumption that the buffalo hides are skinned in the historic manner, as described earlier. It is also figured on large bison hides that are roughly eight feet long, not counting the tail, and about seven feet across. By using the hide placement pattern as discovered on early tipis, it takes approximately eight hides to complete a 12-foot cover, 10 hides to do a 14-foot tipi, 12 for a 16-foot lodge and 14 hides to make an 18-foot tipi.

Each tipi hide weighs about 10 pounds if it is a young bull hide and slightly less if it is a large cow bison. A recent 18 ½- foot tipi I built required 13 ½ hides and weighed about 110 pounds when first set up. After a summer of being outdoors, it lost five pounds due to the drying effects of the sun.

In the days before the horse arrived, tipis were noticeably smaller. Large dogs, similar to huskies, pulled the tipi travois. Elderly Lakota told me that a 14-foot tipi was the common size in the dog days. Twelve poles were used, representing the complete cycle of a year. Each pole had a personal name to identify it without the framework. The smaller tipi size would allow one wife to erect it. The larger tipi of later years, such as an 18-foot lodge, was called a "two-wife tipi." A smaller tipi was easier to heat than a large tipi and lighter for the dogs to pull. Samuel Pond, a missionary in the 1830's, described the early eastern Sioux tipis as being small:

Edward Goodbird is holding his dog travois. Such a device was used to transport a small tipi cover and poles. Horses were also used to pull a similar, but larger framework. (SHSND 0086-1290)

Sewing the Tipi Cover

A Dakota tent or tepee of ordinary size was made of eight dressed buffalo skins, sewed together with sinews, and when set up was of a conical shape, about twelve feet in height, and ten or twelve feet in diameter at the bottom.[4]

One of the earliest visitors to the West was Prince Maximilian. In 1833 he found that the Teton tipis were "generally composed of fourteen skins." With the skins I have access to, this would be an 18 ½-foot tipi. It would be similar to the popular 18-foot canvas tipis seen at today's rendezvous.

Some tipi-makers thought an even number of total hides was preferable while others thought an odd number was better. I have found that it does not matter one way or the other. However, necessity dictates that the first or front row of hides for a Lakota lodge will be an odd number because the first hide

Most tipi construction was a group effort. Once the necessary hides were tanned, the women sewed the tipi using threads from the back muscle (sinew). At the left along the front row of sewn hides there is a buffalo tail. (SHSND 0087-116)

positioned for sewing is the center hide of the first row. It is part of the tie area, near the ear flaps, so it bears considerable weight of the hides connected to it. Therefore it is the largest and thickest hide used in the sewing of the lodge cover. A woman summarized the length of time needed for the construction of a hide tipi:

> The making of the tent skin was one of the most complex technical achievements. It was a major enterprise to get one made, which had to be anticipated at least two years in advance. Eight skins had to be accumulated over four successive hunting periods—a summer hunt, a winter hunt, and on the following year again, a summer and a winter hunt. Sinew of eight buffalo for sewing the skins together also had to be saved. As signs of wear would appear in their tent skin, a woman would remind her husband of their need. Then he would set aside two good skins in each of the four seasons. The average life of a tent skin was no more than ten or twelve years. [5]

Generally the construction of a hide tipi was a group effort overseen by a woman who had earned the right to be a supervisor. The following describes the Lakota guild of tanners:

> An association of women spoken of as tanners (ataha kpo yan pe), but properly tipi-makers, seems to have been a kind of guild. One with a tipi cover to make prepares a feast and sends out a herald to invite all the tipi-makers. When they have assembled, an offering is made and prayers given for the good of all. The skins are then divided out and dressed. Then they are joined and sewed into a tipi cover, etc. It was said, that this served to elevate their craft.[6]

The sewing of a tipi used the same close overlay stitching used for buckskin clothing, except with thicker threads. An awl poked holes through the two edges, and a sinew thread connected the hides. The stitches were less than 1/4 inch apart. Some women used an overhand knot at the end of their sinew threads while others used no knot. In the latter meth-

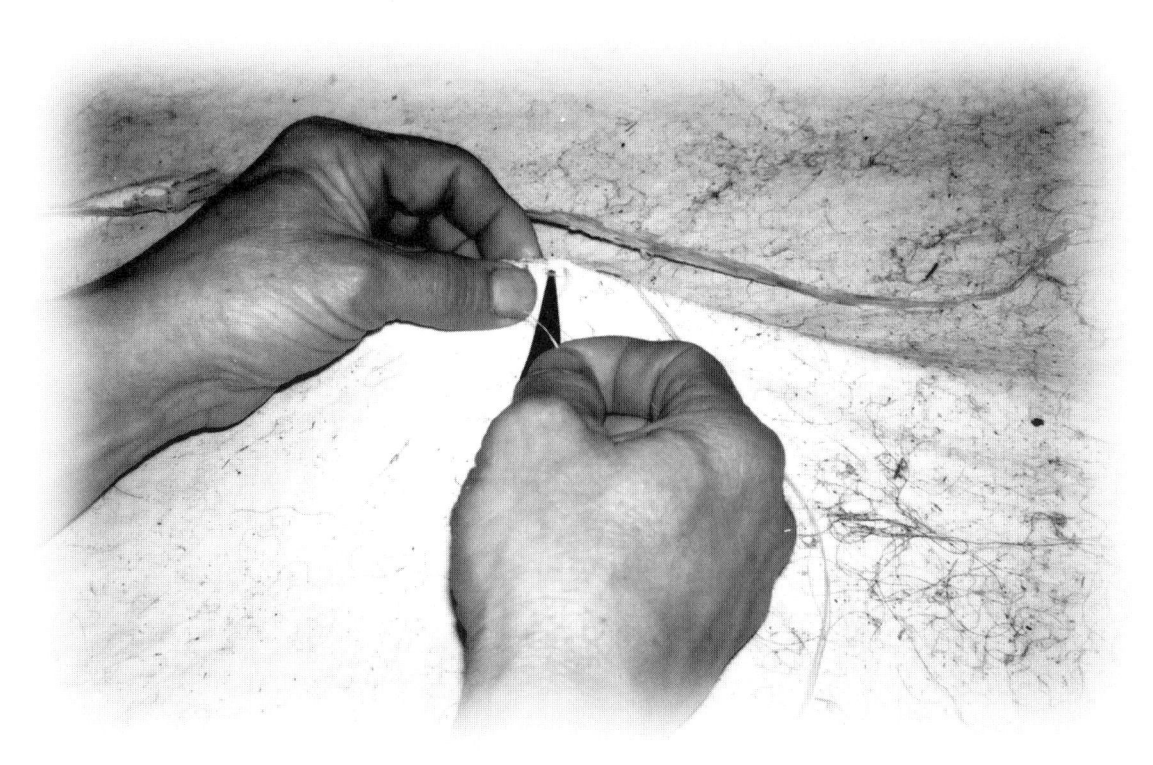

An awl is used to poke holes for sinew sewing

od, the first stitching hole was made, and the sinew thread was pulled through except for the final inch of the tail. The next stitch overlapped the trailing tail of the previous stitch. After the third stitch covered the tail, the end would not pull through, even when it became wet.

Deer sinew threads are approximately 18 inches long, whereas elk or buffalo sinew threads are about two feet long. Buffalo sinews are preferred for sewing because the sewer could attach as much as 14 inches before ending and starting a new thread. At the end a knot was tied or the forward sinew piece was tucked through the last sinew loop. On the tipis I have examined, the trailing ends of the sinew threads all remain intact. The sinew appears unnoticeable because its color blends against the hide color.

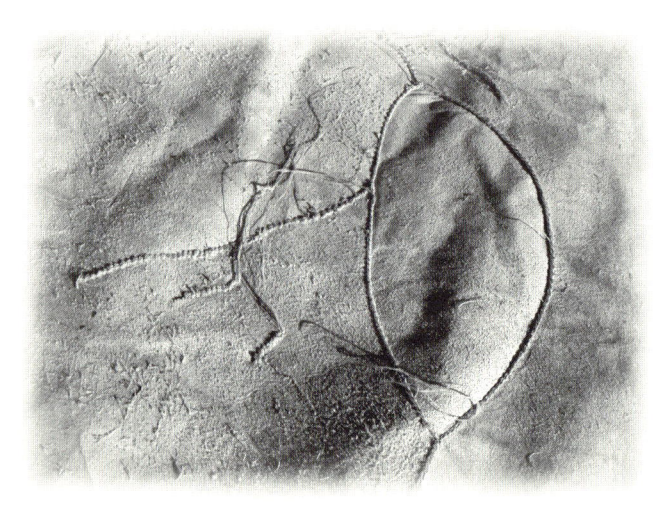

The sewing on the inside of this tipi shows close, tight stitching. The remnant threads are allowed to hang freely.

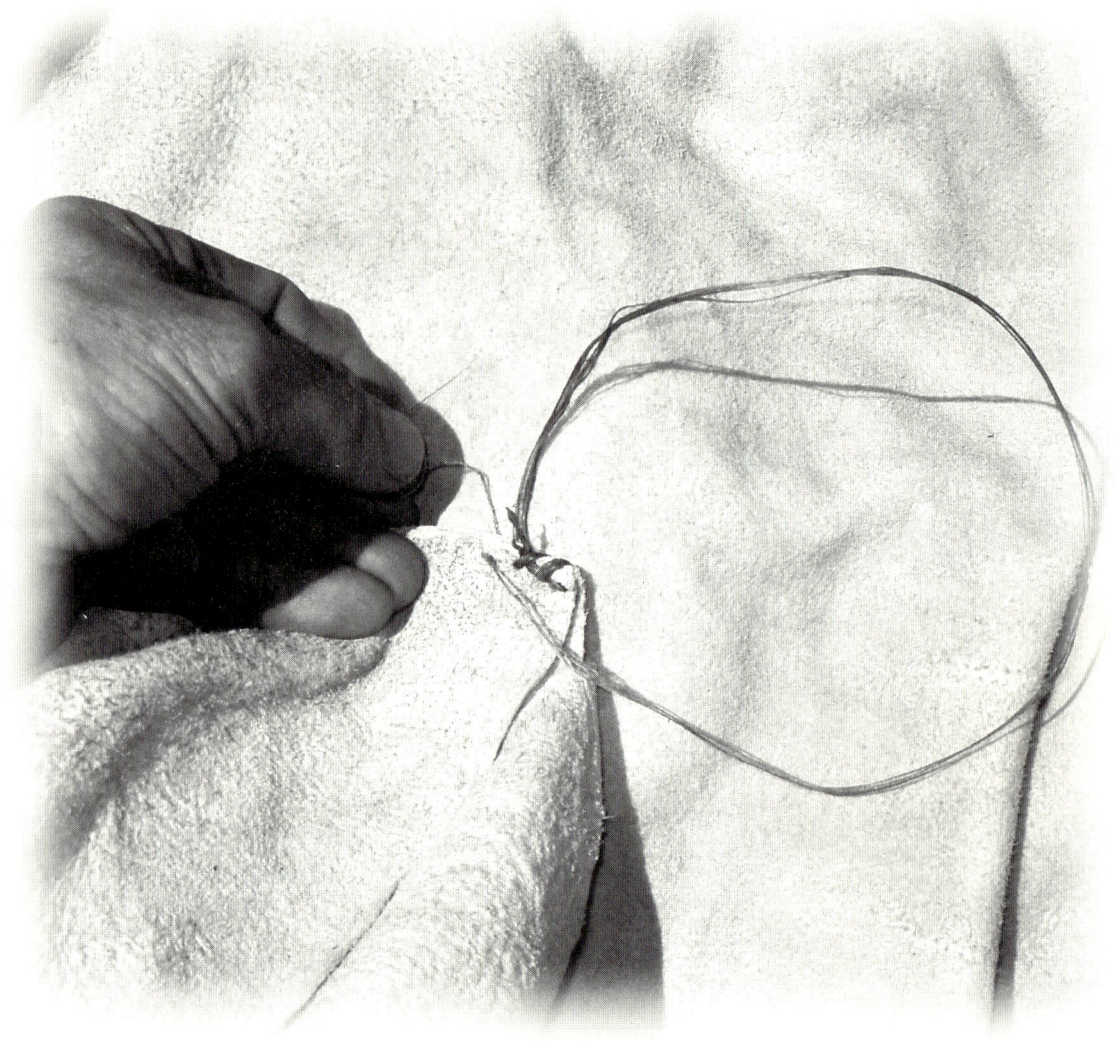

Women often overlapped the tail of a sinew thread to secure the end rather than tying a knot.

The muscle strips along each side of a deer, elk or buffalo's spine was used for sewing threads. After removal of the strips, adhering meat was cleaned from the sinews before drying.

The sinew for sewing threads is found along both sides of the backbone and on top of the tenderloin. It spans from the hip to the shoulder on an animal. The forward part, which has the fine tapered ends for sewing, lies under the shoulder blade. To remove the sinew, a slit is made along the backbone, and a dull blade is inserted between the shiny sinew backstrap tendon and the meat adhering to it. The blade is slid to the hip while pulling up on the sinew strip to free it from the tenderloin. Next the sinew piece is pulled from underneath the shoulder blade and cut at the hip A dull knife scrapes off any meat adhering to the sinew strip. The wet strip is placed on a flat surface to dry, and by the next morning, it should be ready to use.

The back muscle, or sinew, is tough in its ability to secure hides together. I have had tipis outdoors for three years, and most needed no repairs due to broken stitches. The sinew threads are stitched while damp, so as they dry, the stitches conform to the hide. Sinew is slightly elastic, which allows it to stretch before it breaks.

A buffalo hide skinned the old Sioux way is trapezoidal, wide at the rear and tapered to a narrower front. The distance across the front of a buffalo hide is about 6 ½ feet, and the back is about 7 ½ feet across. The hides are fairly straight along their sides when they are skinned by the historic method. The entire front row of tipi hides, except the center one, is placed with rumps along the front edge. The center hide is frequently trimmed narrower at its front to appear somewhat triangular. The hides adjacent to the center hide are placed opposite in their direction to balance out the shape of this center hide. Their wider bases compensate for the first hide's narrowed front. Removing the forward section of the center hide eliminates its weaker front legs and belly hide to retain the strongest part of this hide. This section bears the weight of the cover.

In research I could identify the position of hides within a cover in various ways. The direction of some hides were indicated by the darker color of the hump and backbone and, of course, by any tails. Without these aids the swallow tail dangles reveal where the front legs were. This allowed me to see the placement of each hide. Using these visual guides, I found that it is not just the Sioux who use the pattern lay-out that I illustrate; the Arapaho, Cheyenne, Comanche, Northern Apache and Ute do also.

A hide skinned by the pre-reservation method was trapezoidal—narrow at the front and wide at the rear. This shape permitted tribes to sew buffalo hides using the pattern as described in this book.

SEWING THE TIPI COVER

A hide patch was added to fill a gap where the fronts of four buffalo hides converged.

These are Apache Indians from Ft. Sill, Oklahoma. They have followed the same pattern for sewing a tipi as used by the Sioux. Directly above the heads of the seated persons the dark line of a buffalo's back can be seen. The front of this hide meets another hide head-to-head at the right. Midway at the right edge of this picture a circular patch has been sewn to fill a gap where four hides converge. A boy at the doorway is holding a hair-on buffalo door cover. (SHSND 0014-033)

LACING PINS

Tipi lacing pins, used to close the front of the tipi, were usually made from chokecherry. Lacing pins were about fifteen inches long and the thickness of a pencil. The outer portion of the pins usually had rings carved into the bark. It is surprising that such a delicate pin could support the heavy weight of a hide lodge. Seldom did chokecherry pins break, although they often warped from the strain of holding together the two sides of the tipi.

Making the slits for receiving the skewers was apparently done after the cover was put in place the first time because the vertical holes are randomly six to nine inches apart. There are double holes on the right side of the tipi's front that match double slits on the left. A few historic tipis have single holes along their right edge to facilitate the pinning. One early drawing by Rudolph Kurz shows the front lacing on an Iowa tipi running vertically rather than horizontally.

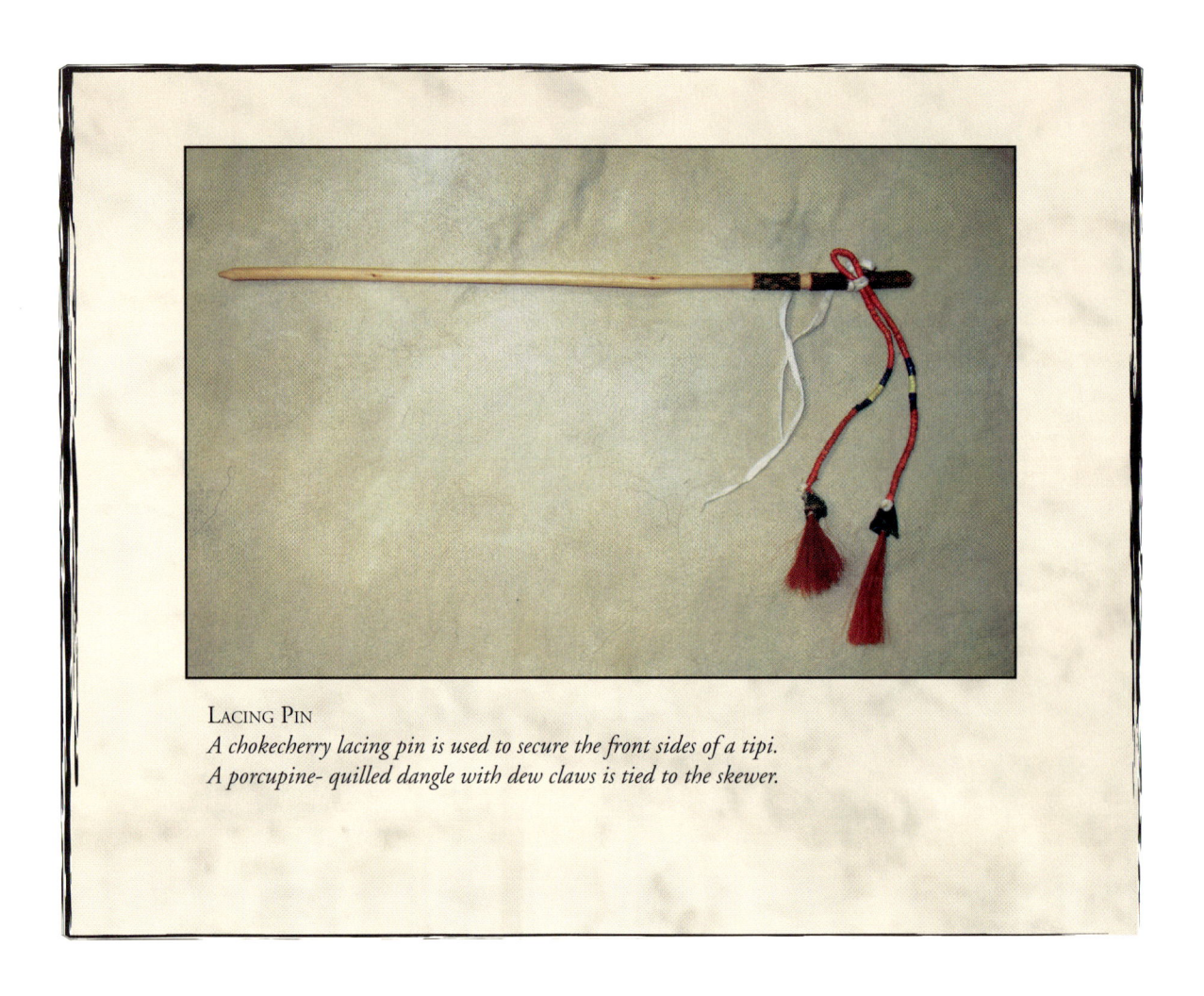

LACING PIN
A chokecherry lacing pin is used to secure the front sides of a tipi. A porcupine-quilled dangle with dew claws is tied to the skewer.

LACING PINS

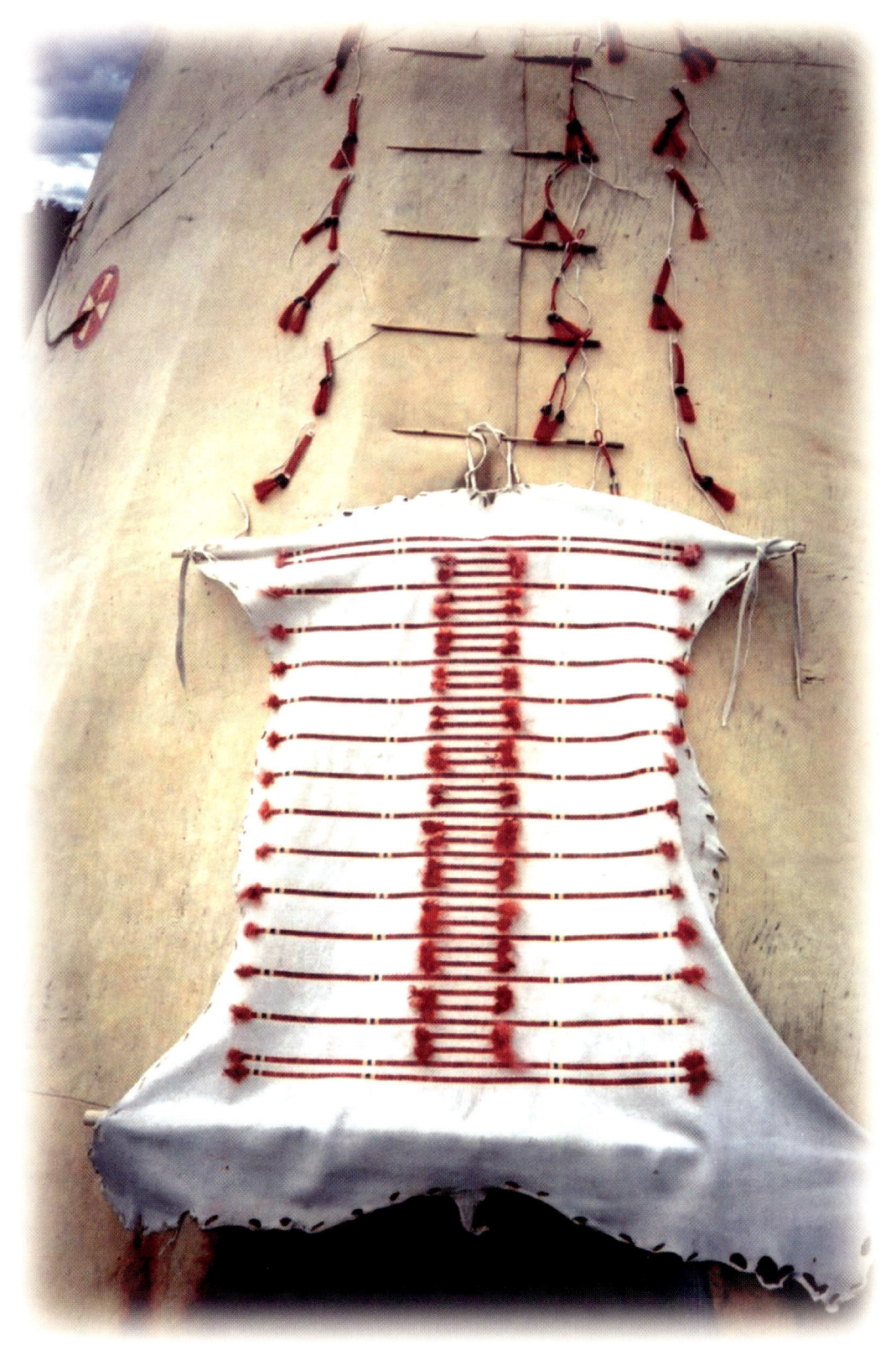

The Lakota women were noted for their elaborate use of porcupine quillwork to decorate their tipi homes. Seen here are decorated lacing pins and a door cover.

DECORATIONS ON A TIPI

It is difficult to find painted lodges in pictures of early Sioux encampments. If there was a painted tipi, it was usually a society lodge using an image of the animal power depicted on the lodge. One early explorer said that only one tipi out of twelve was painted. Among tribes such as the Kiowa or Blackfeet, painted tipis were more common, especially as commercial paints became available. McClintock (in The Old North Trail) said that in a camp of 350 Blackfeet lodges, there were 35 painted tipis.

The lack of painted tipis was partly attributed to the large quantity of earth pigment needed to cover the large surface of a tipi cover. Also, earth colors readily smudged onto unpainted areas. Another problem was that painted areas blocked the light. The Institute of the Range and American Mustang wanted ten canvas lodges they owned to be painted. They thought it would be great to "spruce up the camp" with painted lodges. Using watered-down latex paint, they colored the tops, bottoms and midsections of all their tipis. The result was that the interiors were so dark during the day that a flashlight was needed in order to see.

This ceremonial lodge has painted pipes near the doorway and many sunbursts on the cover. Two rosettes with dangles are visible on this side of the tipi. A horsetail ornament is hanging from the extended lifting pole. (SHSND A1013)

Decorations on a Tipi

A woman is sewing porcupine quills to buckskin. (SHSND 0039-50)

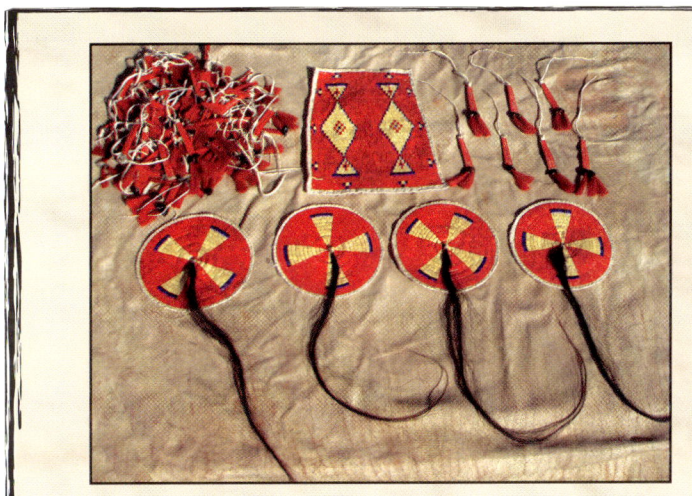

Decorations
These are red-dyed porcupine quilled decorations for a hide tipi: At the upper left and right are tinklers with dew claws. The center item is an ownership insignia. The bottom row shows four rosettes with horsetail centers.

Decorations on a Tipi

In lieu of painting, the Lakota wife who was ambitious embellished her tipi with porcupine-quilled or beaded circles. These rosettes, called "stars," were sewn in four quadrants around the exterior of the tipi. These represented the four directions. Red-dyed porcupine quilled tinklers also decorated the outer edges of the smoke flaps. Additionally, there often were two lanes of red porcupine-quilled dangles down the back of the tipi starting below the quilled ownership insignia.

The rear of this tipi cover shows a buffalo skin with its tail intact. A porcupine quilled ownership insignia is at the top and rows of quilled tinklers adorn the back.

Decorations on a Tipi

Directly below the tipi tie area was the important quillwork (later beaded) design which identified the owner of the lodge. This insignia piece was usually trapezoidal in shape among the Sioux but circular among the Cheyenne and Mandan. It resolved any disputes about the ownership of a tipi. Mix-ups regarding ownership of lodges occurred after the tipis were rolled up and the women gathered their travois horses. When the cover was tied to the lifting pole, the insignia design would verify the correct lodge owner in the event of a mix-up. The insignia piece was a separate decorated piece stitched onto the tipi. This added piece also served the function of reinforcing the tie region. Lakota and Cheyenne called this emblem piece "the sun."

A common practice among many Sioux, Cheyenne and Assiniboine was to cut serration along the edges of the ear flaps. This practice was abandoned when canvas lodges were made since pinking the ear flaps unraveled the cotton material.

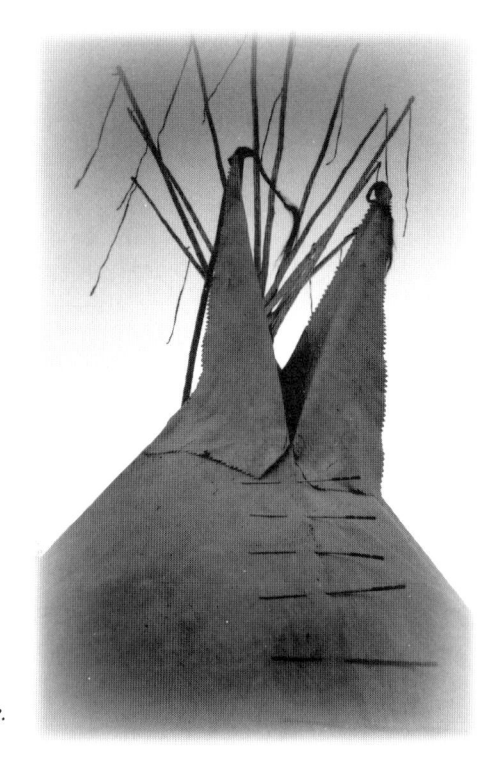

Many hide tipis had serrated ear flaps. This lodge also has buckskin streams at the tip of each pole.

These are fully decorated tipis with painted war exploits, beaded rosettes with drops, tinklers along the front flaps and down the back of the lodges, owner insignias at the upper back and a tail on a lifting pole. (SHSND 0739-v1-p54)

Decorations on a Tipi

The Sioux and other tribes identified the owner of a lodge by the design of the quilled or beaded insignia below the tie flap.

GROUND PEGS

The common pegs used to secure the tipi cover to the ground were made of a hard wood, usually ash or chokecherry. Often the bark was left on the upper part of the stake to provide strength and deter splitting. The tops were slightly dome-shaped. This prevented the tops from flaring out when they were hammered. Most stakes were 18 inches long and slightly over an inch thick. They were driven at a slant through a two inch slit every two feet around the bottom of the hide cover. In photographs it appears the cover was staked close to the ground, except in hot weather when one side of the tipi cover was raised for a draft. In the summer the liners that typically hung on the inside of the lodge were draped around the outside of the poles to provide shade.

A tipi is pinned to the ground using stakes driven through slits near the bottom of the hide cover.

The many meat racks shows a successful hunt in this camp near the Yellowstone River. The tipi in the center has a travois resting against the back side. The tipi to the right has a stretched and dried hide propped on its cover. At the lower right is a child's play tipi. (SHSND 0087-100)

When the camp was on the move and the ground was hard or frozen, securing the tipi's base with wooden stakes was usually impossible. Without pegs, the base of the tipi was sometimes held down with rocks. Whenever stakes could be driven into the ground, logs were also placed above the pegged section to prevent the wind from lifting the cover from the pegs. The logs also provided a convenient place to sit around the tipi.

The heavy rocks left behind called "tipi rings" are typically flat stones placed inside the tipi and in front of the tipi poles. These keep the framework of poles from being pushed inward by gusts of wind. During winter weather, rocks on the exterior holding the leather bottom to the ground would eventually freeze the skirt to the ground and make the tipi immovable until a spring thaw. The use of logs to hold down the tipi's base is told here:

> Since the ground was still frozen, tent pins could not be used; instead, small logs were laid along the bottom of the tent upon the edge of the tent skins.[9]

Logs were placed on tipi pegs to prevent wind from lifting the cover from the stakes. A horse travois is leaning against the side of this tipi. Many buffalo tails decorate this cover. (SHSND A0971)

A circle of rocks used to anchor a tipi is called a "tipi ring." Although stones were thrown aside when this camp moved, parts of several rings are still evident.

In the foreground Eat Dog and his son are sitting on the tipi cover. The fortified door coverings in the background indicate that this is a winter camp. (SDSHS, Morrow)

TIPI POLES

The tree preferred for tipi poles is the lodgepole pine. This variety of pine grows in heavy stands with trees several feet apart. A forest fire aids seeds in the cone to loosen and fall out. The fire kills competing trees, allowing the heavy seed concentration of the lodgepole pine to produce a dense stand. Most lodgepoles are harvested in Montana and Wyoming.

Because the lodgepole tree stands are dense, there are few low limbs. Dense forest stands have only a few sprigs of greenery at the tree's top. This was a convenient tree for native tribes to use for poles since the lodgepole trees are slender and straight and have few limbs to remove.

Many lodgepole trees used for tipis are about 25 feet tall and only three to four inches across at their base. They have a spiral twist to the grain, which makes them strong. Using primitive tools, it was easy for tribes to cut and debark the trees without needing to reduce the thickness of the tree trunks.

A tree weighs about 40 pounds and steams on a summer day when the bark is removed. After several weeks the same pole weighs about 10 to 15 pounds, depending on the length of the pole.

In museum collections of tipis, the bases of tipi poles have long tapers, starting about 18 inches from the bottoms. This shaping occurred naturally as the poles were pulled on the travois. The pointed bottoms were necessary for inserting into the ground to keep the poles from moving during a storm. Bird Woman describes how the poles were carried on each side of a horse:

> The poles, ten, twelve, or thirteen in number, were strung together by a thong through holes pierced at their smaller ends.[7]

A tall tipi does not require thicker poles. Once I ordered a set of lodgepoles for an 18-foot hide tipi. The logger said, "I did you a favor; I didn't give you any of those skinny poles." When I arrived to load the poles, I saw massive lodgepoles about five or six inches across at their bottoms. I took the skinniest poles and left the remaining poles in a tree, where they likely still remain. Rather than using thick poles, the Plains tribes used more poles in the foundation for strength. These poles were narrow where they crossed at the neck of the tipi. This gave the cover a snug fit, and rain would seldom drip into the lodge. Years ago, a customer bought a large bison hide tipi from me and set it up at a national rendezvous in Montana. It was an 18-foot tipi tied with eighteen narrow poles using a hide rope. It rained steadily for five days, and the buyer said it was the only tipi around that was dry inside. Selecting lodgepoles is explained below:

> The best poles are straight as an arrow, smooth, pointed neatly at the butts, and seasoned so as not to sag under the weight of the tent covering. In use, they soon become coated with a protective varnish of shining soot, and will last for years…In length, the poles measure fifteen to thirty feet; in greatest thickness, two to four inches… In general, one may say that there is a pole for every thirty inches of circumference. Of course, the more poles, the stauncher the tipi.[8]

Tipi Poles

The Lakota refer to the spiral of tipi poles as "a nest."

TWO-WIFE TIPI
About 18' Tall

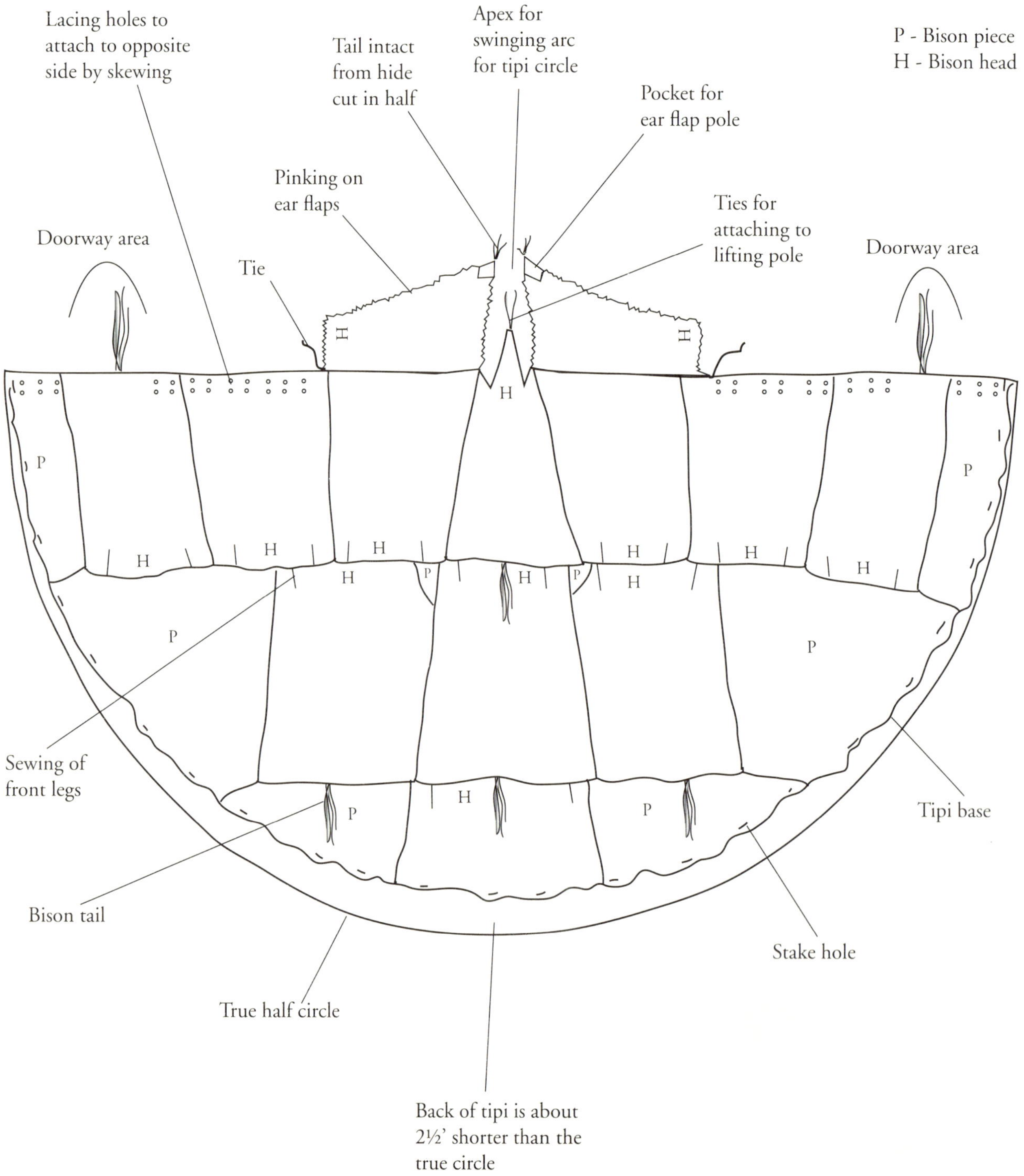

Lacing holes to attach to opposite side by skewing

Tail intact from hide cut in half

Apex for swinging arc for tipi circle

Pocket for ear flap pole

P - Bison piece
H - Bison head

Pinking on ear flaps

Ties for attaching to lifting pole

Doorway area

Tie

Doorway area

Sewing of front legs

Tipi base

Bison tail

Stake hole

True half circle

Back of tipi is about 2½' shorter than the true circle

ERECTING THE HIDE TIPI

The early tipis of the Lakota (Teton), Cheyenne, Arapaho and Assiniboine used a three-pole foundation, or tripod. The Crow and Blackfoot used a four-pole foundation. The Crow were usually enemies of the Lakota, so it was important to discern from a distance whether a village was friendly or not by the arrangement of the poles and shape of the smoke flaps. Among the early Lakota lodges, one or two eagle feathers were hung from the lifting pole to help identify their villages from afar. The respected ethnologist Clark Wissler compares the Lakota (Teton) to other tribes in the manner of setting up a tipi:

> The [Cheyenne] poles are arranged as a tripod, one leg to the left of the door, as among the Teton, around which are nine other poles. The whole arrangement of the poles is like that of the Teton. However, all the poles except the one by which the cover is raised, are bound by the cord. An Assiniboine model is similar to the above in construction, except that the forward leg of the tripod is to the right of the door…The third pole of the tripod always forms the left side of the door as one enters the tipi, so they begin to fill in with the balance of the poles to the right of this one, then to the left and last at the back. When all the poles are in place, the long end of the rope is wrapped several times around the tops of the poles to bind them securely together, and tied to the north tripod pole, or to a stake near the centre of the tipi floor, if the wind blows hard. As to the Arapaho women, I find that their way is exactly the same as that of the Cheyenne.[10]

After the hide tipi was set up for the first time, the ear flaps were closed, and the interior was smoked for several hours to make it water-resistant. The smoking prevented the hides, upon becoming wet, from being stiff after drying. Smoking was the final step to complete the tanning process. Smoke readily adhered to the hide so the fibers became set in their position. It was easier to smoke the entire tipi than to smoke each hide separately. The following describes the procedure:

> When the cover was cut and sewn, it was stretched over its frame, the smoke flaps were closed, and the inside was cured with heavy smoke scented with sagebrush to keep it supple, waterproof, and fragrant.[11]

The Lakota commonly honored great warriors by inviting them to walk across the cover to bless it after it was sewn. Now the lodge was ready to be set up after measurements were obtained. The first measuring determined where to tie the three foundation poles. Assuming the door opening will face east, you begin by fully opening the hide cover and placing the back north and south poles along the center of the cover, allowing three inches to extend beyond the bottom

SMOKED HIDE
This is a magnified view showing the fibers of a smoked, brain-tanned hide. Creosote from smoke coats hide fibers to enable a hide to dry soft after being wetted.

To establish the tie point for the three foundation poles, the back poles (north and south) are placed down the center of the cover and marked where they meet the base of the tie area (located between the ear flaps). The door pole is placed one-third of the distance between the door of the cover and the north and south poles and is also marked where it meets the base of the tie flap.

This shows the north and south poles with the door pole on top. They are pre-tied with a short thong where they meet the base of the tie flap.

edge. This extra length allowed for later inserting the pointed bottoms into the ground. A mark was placed on the poles indicating where they met the base of the tie flap. The measurements for pole lengths for the two back poles, known as the north and south poles, vary:

Pole length for a
 twelve-foot lodge is 10 feet, 2 inches.
Pole length for a
 fourteen-foot lodge is 11 feet, 9 inches.
Pole length for a
 sixteen-foot lodge is 13 feet, 11 inches.
Pole length for an
 eighteen-foot lodge is 15 feet, 11 inches.

It might appear strange that the measurements for tying the north and south poles do not match the size of the tipi. The stated size is not the height to where the poles cross, but the measurement from the highest point between the ear flaps to the ground by the door.

Next, the door pole was placed 1/3 of the distance between the front edge of the cover and the previously measured north and south poles. The measurements for the door pole vary:

The pole length for a
 twelve-foot lodge was 11 feet.
The pole length for a
 fourteen-foot lodge was 13 feet, 1 inch.
The pole length for a
 sixteen-foot lodge was 15 feet, 3 inches.
The pole length for an
 eighteen-foot lodge was 17 feet, 1 inch.

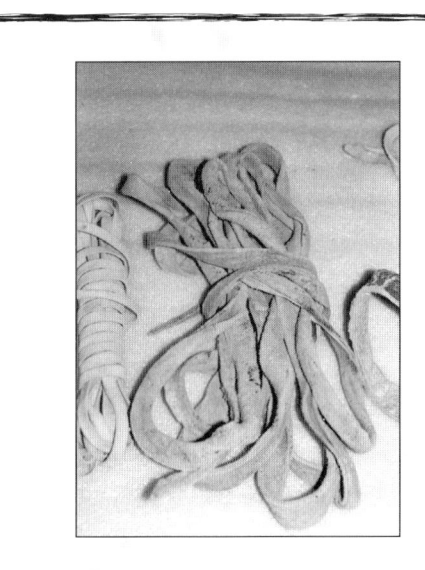

ROPE
The typical lashing for tying the tipi poles was a one-inch, flat buffalo rawhide rope. Braided rawhide and hair ropes were also used.

The poles are placed as they were positioned on the cover during measuring. Stakes identify the places for the door, south and north pole after the tripod is raised. The door pole is located beside the antler hammer and faces east.

The three poles (north, south and door) were tied where they had been marked using a clove hitch. The ropes used were of flat or braided bison rawhide or braided horsehair.

To lock the tripod so it would not fall when set upright, the north pole was carried to a north position while the tie rope pulled the tripod upward. With a large tipi, this task was accomplished by two wives working together. While one woman pulled the rope, the other carried the north pole to its new place, without moving either the south or door poles. The final distances between the tripod bases were critical because all the other poles rest on the three foundation poles. If the distances between the tripod poles were incorrect, the cover would not fit properly. The following tripod measurements indicate the distances between poles:

A twelve-foot tipi was 8'10" between the north and south poles and 10'5" from each of these to the door pole.

A fourteen-foot tipi was 10'3" between the north and south poles and 11'6" from each of these to the door pole.

A sixteen-foot tipi was 12' between the north and south poles and 13'6" from each of these to the door pole.

An eighteen-foot tipi was 13' between the north and south poles and 16' from each of these to the door pole.

The tipi is a tilted cone with the front longer than the back. This accounts for the door pole distances being longer than the distances between the south and north poles at the rear of the tipi. The Plains Indians wanted the back of the tipi to be steep to brace the back of the tipi to the westerly winds. The shape also permitted more headroom inside the tipi and put the fireplace forward of center to allow space at the back of the lodge.

The tied foundation poles are lifted while the north pole (lying along the south pole) is carried to the peg indicated for it. Moving the north pole tightens the wrap of the poles and locks the tripod.

Erecting the Hide Tipi

Next came the placing of lodge poles into the tripod. There were three arrangements for the positioning of poles into the tipi framework. The procedure I was taught appears to be consistent with historic practices and is verified by the poles seen in old photographs. This pattern results in a tight cluster of poles at the throat, giving little opportunity for rain to run down the poles during a storm.

The tipi is a tilted cone with the back of the tipi shorter and steeper than the long sloping front. This shape helped brace the back of the tipi to westerly winds.

TIPI POLE ORDER

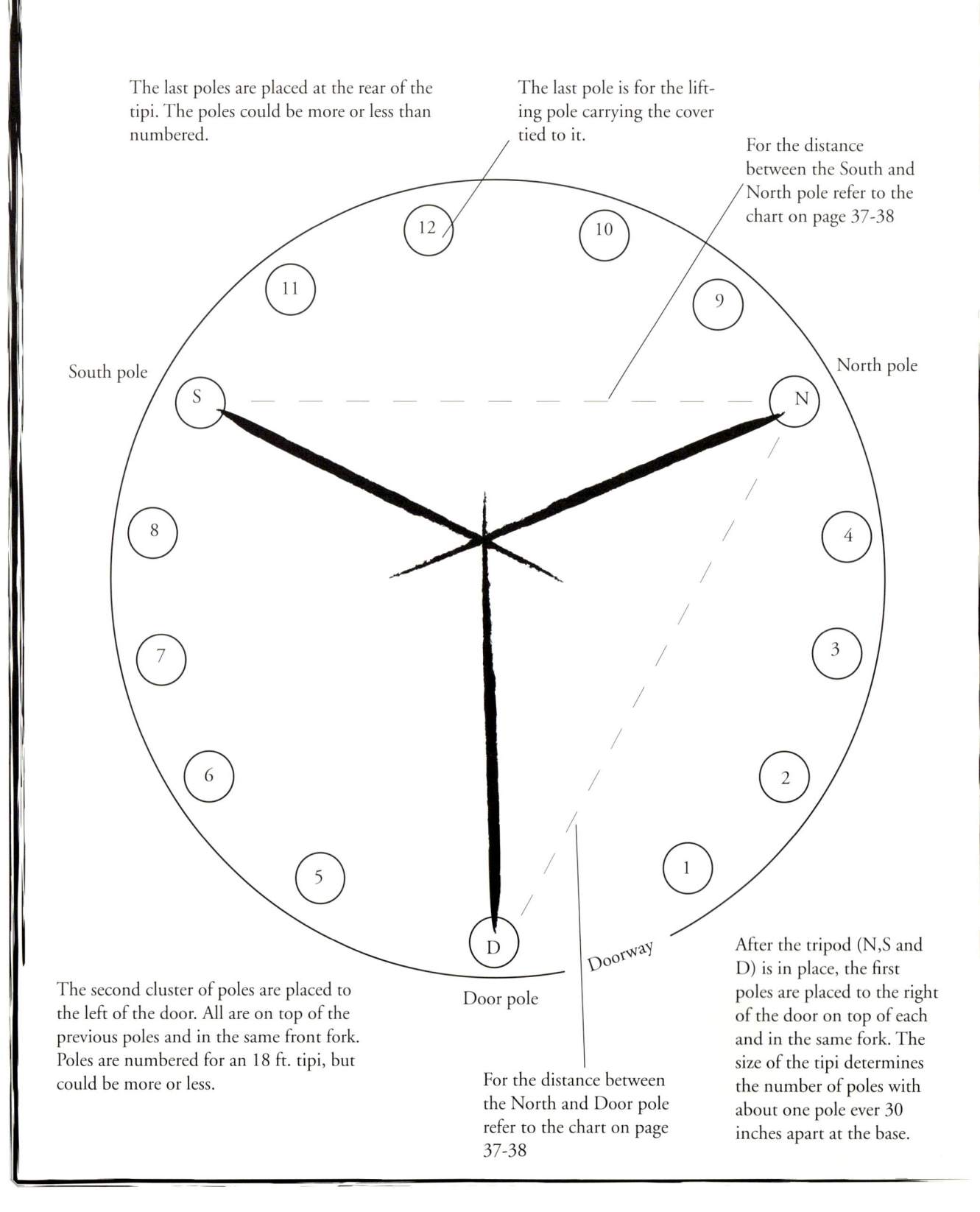

The last poles are placed at the rear of the tipi. The poles could be more or less than numbered.

The last pole is for the lifting pole carrying the cover tied to it.

For the distance between the South and North pole refer to the chart on page 37-38

South pole

North pole

After the tripod (N, S and D) is in place, the first poles are placed to the right of the door on top of each and in the same fork. The size of the tipi determines the number of poles with about one pole ever 30 inches apart at the base.

The second cluster of poles are placed to the left of the door. All are on top of the previous poles and in the same front fork. Poles are numbered for an 18 ft. tipi, but could be more or less.

Door pole

Doorway

For the distance between the North and Door pole refer to the chart on page 37-38

ERECTING THE HIDE TIPI

The first pole is placed into the front fork to the right of the door pole.

The second pole is placed to the right of the previous pole.

The placement of poles is accomplished from three sides beginning to the right of the door pole (facing the tipi). The first pole is placed several feet to the right of the door pole into the front fork. The second pole is also placed in the front fork on top of the previous pole. The third pole is placed on top of the second in the same cluster. For a small tipi, this completes the filling in of the right side of the front fork. The distances between the poles is estimated to be about equal distances apart since they can be adjusted later. For larger tipis more poles are added into the same front fork so there is a pole about every thirty inches. All the poles are placed upon the previous pole, creating a spiral pattern.

Each successive pole, continuing to the right, is placed on top of the one before. Depending on the size of the tipi, three to six poles are placed in this fork. For this tipi six poles have been stacked to the right of the door.

The next set of poles is placed to the left of the door pole (facing the tipi). These are also laid in order with each succeeding pole on top of the one before it. The first pole is placed several feet to the left of the door. This pole will be on top of the previous right side cluster. The next pole will be several feet to the left of the base of the previous pole and staked on top of the previous pole. The placing of poles on this side continues to the left and will be the same number of poles as those placed on the right side, all in the same front fork to present a spiral pattern.

The last cluster of poles is placed at the rear of the tipi. In the back fork, there is an obvious gap where the final set of poles will be placed. When looking at the opening, the first lodgepole is placed several feet to the right of the north pole and each pole is stacked on top of the previous one, continuing toward the south pole. The number of poles used at the rear of the tipi

The second cluster of poles is begun to the left of the door pole and continues to the left. The first pole has been added to the left of the door on top of the poles from the other side.

The poles to the left of the door pole have been stacked.

At the rear of the tipi, the poles are placed into the empty area of the rear fork, starting at the left side (when facing the tipi) and working to the right.

ERECTING THE HIDE TIPI 43

This is an upward view from inside the tipi showing the poles to the right and left of the doorway in the front fork. The open area at the back will have poles added later into the back fork.

The number of poles added to the back will vary according to the size of the tipi. The center position at the rear is reserved for the lifting pole.

usually is the same as the number placed to the right or left of the door. Sometimes one less pole is used because the north and south poles are closer to each other than each is to the door. The center position at the rear of the tipi is skipped to be filled in later with the lifting pole after the poles were wrapped.

The rope used to tie the tripod was now wrapped four times, the sacred number to the Lakota. The winding of the rope started beside the south pole and, after four wraps, ended after the north pole. During the wrapping of the cluster of poles, the rope was pulled hard to cinch the cluster since this wrapping holds the poles down in a storm.

ERECTING THE HIDE TIPI

All the framework poles are in place except the lifting pole which is on the ground.

The lodgepoles have been tied and the cover has been opened for measuring the lifting pole

The poles are secured with four wraps, the sacred number to the Lakota. The wrapping of the poles is in a clockwise, or "sunwise," direction. (SHSND 0200-278)

Erecting the Hide Tipi

The next step is to measure the lifting pole. A stout pole is placed down the center of the tipi cover and marked where it meets the top of the tie flap. In addition to a mark or groove to identify the tying pole, a short antler wedge is often driven into the pole at the marked point. This easily identifies the lifting pole and stops the tied cover from sliding down when the cover is set in place. Additionally, the tip of the pole often has tied to it a buffalo tail or object to identify the lodge. When the lifting pole is in place, this emblem draped above the entrance of the tipi. The High Dog winter count for 1801 mentions a new rule decided upon by a democratic gathering of Sioux as follows:

The lifting pole is measured along the back of the tipi with three inches extending beyond the cover and tied to thongs at the top of the tie flap. Antler pegs keep the cover from sliding when it is lifted.

The Sioux established a rule in 1801 that only a chief could have a horse tail suspended from the lifting pole. Such a pole was usually extra-long, allowing the emblem to drape above the doorway. This tipi has a log holding the bottom of the cover. A buffalo head is painted near the bottom of the cover with a lightning bolt extending upward. (SHSND 0087-0095)

ERECTING THE HIDE TIPI

This buffalo hide cover weighs slightly over a hundred pounds. It has been tied to the lifting pole and is being raised to a place at the center in the back fork. A rock placed at the base of this pole keeps it from sliding while being lifted.

The lifting pole with the tied-on cover has been set into the fork at the rear of the tipi.

And at this meeting the horsetail badge was adopted as an insignia for a ruler (if a man, not if a woman). Note that the horse had become now important to the Sioux though only a portion of them had horses as yet. Note also that the horse was a sacred animal.[12]

A large tipi was called a "two wife tipi," partly due to the work of tanning a considerable number of hides but mainly because it took the muscle of several women to lift the tipi cover. When two women worked together, one placed her foot at the bottom of the lifting pole to keep it from sliding while the other woman started near the end of the pole and walked it upward and into the back fork. One person could walk the lifting pole into position in the back fork if a heavy, flat rock was used as a fulcrum.

After the cover was laid into the back fork, each half of the cover was pulled around to the front. Buffalo tails were used as handles to pull the cover around. The back row of hides (with their tails intact) identified the center of the back, making it simple to determine each half to pull to the front. The tipi halves met at the doorway between the door pole and the adjacent pole toward the north. To hold the two halves together for pinning, there were two thongs below the smoke flaps to tie before beginning the pinning. Sometimes the tails by the doorway were tied to serve as a ladder rung to reach the topmost lacing holes. Other times a small

The right and left halves of the buffalo hide cover have been brought to the front. The tails of the doorway have been tied to hold the sides together. A pole has been lashed across the doorway to make a ladder to reach the upper lacing holes.

child was hoisted up to begin the pinning, or a temporary ladder was made by lashing a stout pole across the door poles.

The securing of the front halves of the tipi involved inserting lacing pins through double holes on the left (facing the tipi) matching with double holes on the right. Some old tipis used single holes on the underside, which simplified the pinning. These holes were usually from seven to nine inches apart along the front of the tipi, except where the doorway was located. To allow easy entry into the tipi in warm weather the two or three lacing holes below the door were not pinned. Tipis of historic times had no cut-out doorway. Without a large cut-out hole, it was easier to keep the door flap in place. Many varieties of door covers were used. It did not seem important what was used, as long as it stopped the wind and rain from blowing into the lodge.

Next the ear flaps were secured with poles into the corner pockets. Tribes other than the Lakota, such as the Cheyenne, also had corner pockets on their smoke flaps. The Arapaho used a three-pole foundation like the Sioux but omitted the pockets in their ear flaps. They instead used a hole at the upper edge of each smoke flap. A pocket or hole in the corner of the smoke flap was an indicator of a tipi's tribal identity.

After the ear flap pockets were secured, the base of the two poles was carried to the rear of the tipi. Some groups crossed the butts of the poles, which caused the front opening of the tipi to be spread wide. Others did not cross their poles but had the bottoms touch. Of course, the poles were pushed forward to make the ear flaps taut. In bad weather the smoke poles were brought to the front and crossed. In the summer there was not too much concern about the appearance of the smoke flaps, as can be seen from old photographs. Cooking was done outdoors in warm weather so there was no need to adjust the flaps to control the smoke.

Wood is placed at the entrance to hold down the tipi cover and provide ready access to firewood. (This is a double image for a stereoscope.) (SHSND A3858)

Erecting the Hide Tipi

The skewer is connecting two holes on the left side of the entrance through two holes on the right. The pinning will continue down the front, except for the doorway.

This Sioux tipi has a pole in each corner pocket. A buffalo tail extends from the tip of each pocket.

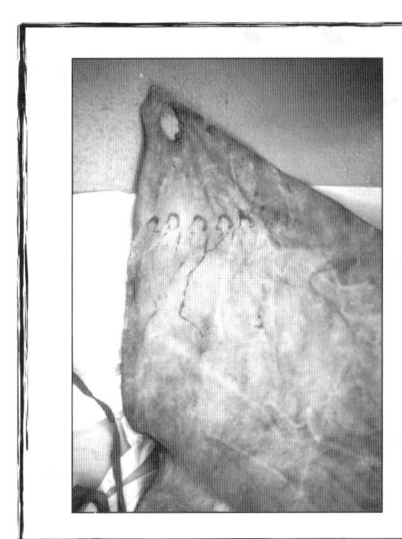

Hole
Some tribes, such as the Crow and Arapaho, had no corner pockets on their ear flaps. They placed smoke poles through a hole in the corners of their smoke flaps. (SHSND 15029-5)

Each smoke flap has a corner pocket where a pole will be inserted. The poles regulate the flaps to control the draft for a fire and close the smoke hole.

Erecting the Hide Tipi

The ear flap poles are placed at the rear of the tipi in calm weather. Before a storm or when leaving a camp, the poles are brought to the front and overlapped to close the smoke hole. This tipi has the back rolled up to get a breeze from the west (tipis generally faced the east). Along the back cover are quilled dangles. (SDSHS)

In the summertime the cooking was done outside; therefore ear flap poles were frequently not put in place. This tipi owner has maintained the tradition of not cutting out a doorway. (SDSHS)

After the cover was pinned, the pole bases were buried several inches into the ground. This kept the tipi from "walking in the wind."

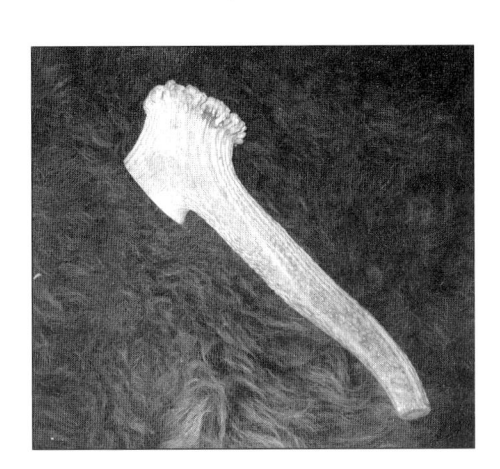

HAMMER
The brow-tine horn of an elk was often used as a hammer for staking a tipi cover to the ground.

Now the lodge poles inside the tipi, except for the tripod, were gradually pushed out to fill out the circle of the tipi. Then, beside each pole, a shallow opening was made into which the base of each pole was dropped. This kept the tipi poles from sliding inward from the wind.

The final step in setting up the tipi was pegging the cover to the ground. The pounder of preference for this task was an elkhorn hammer. A large rock could also serve the purpose of driving in the tipi stakes. It was necessary to slant the pegs so the wind would not slide the cover off the stakes.

In the late fall, villages were set up in river bottoms where there was a good supply of trees and water and there weren't strong winds. Generally, a camp did not relocate during cold weather but waited until springtime arrived. Samuel Pond describes the problems presented if a camp moved in cold weather:

On arrival at the camping ground, there was much to be done and little time in which to do it. If the snow were deep and the cold intense, many of the party must suffer severely. Fires were built on the ground, and children were wrapped in skins and blankets, but could not be made comfortable till the tepees were pitched, so that many of them were often crying with cold and hunger. In the meantime the women had their hands full. The snow was to be removed and the ground to be leveled, if it was rough. This work must be done with a hoe, a difficult and tedious operation, when the ground is hard frozen and the mercury below zero, as the writer can well remember…Fourteen tepee poles were to be found and dragged often a considerable distance through the snow, making two or three heavy loads for a strong woman. The tent was then erected, and dry grass cut up from some swamp was brought and put all around the tent or tepee on the outside, for the Indian women would not bank their tents with snow lest it should melt and injure the tent. Hay was also strewn inside to spread the beds on, for the frozen ground was hard and cold. Then wood was brought for the fire, very dry for they burn no other. Last of all, water was brought and hung over the fire to warm or cook the supper…[13]

The owner of this tipi is gone so the flaps are closed and the door "locked" with crossed sticks. (SDSHS)

This is a winter camp of Chief Spotted Eagle near the Tongue River in Montana. A woman is standing in front of a buffalo hide which is draped over the frame. To her right is another buffalo hide. (SHSND 0410-139)

THE BUFFALO HIDE LINER

The liner is an inside tipi curtain used mainly to provide an air space as insulation during cold weather. In Lakota it is called "ozan," meaning "curtain." A suspended hide ceiling, used in winter to reduce the area to be heated, is called "tiozan." Some books call this ceiling an "ozan," but the old Lakota all agree that it is the liner curtain that is correctly called an ozan.

The early buffalo hide liners that I have examined were made using two hides connecting rump to rump. This I could determine by looking for the swallowtail dangles, which for a liner are on the inner surface of a hide. The majority of liners have a small wedge-shaped insert added between the two hides. The triangle insert caused the hides to have a slight v-slant that fitted the ozan to the inside curve of the tipi. Each panel section was slightly over six feet tall and thirteen feet long. It would take three or four ozan panels to encircle the tipi. In warm weather only one or two liners might be used or sometimes none at all. Long liner panels encircling half of the tipi's interior seems to be a reservation innovation when the villages were no longer constantly on the move.

The tipi cover has been removed, permitting a view of a liner or ozan belonging to Mrs. American Horse. (SDSHS)

The group of women is sewing a new tipi for the one in the background. This permits a view of a liner in the background which has been placed on the outer side poles to make a shade. (SDSHS)

The early hide liner or ozan was fairly quick to install. Sections were tied to a rope that encircled the poles and were not laboriously tied along the bottom to each lodgepole, as is done today. Instead, flat rocks and household articles were placed on the liner's base to hold it back at a slant and keep the tipi poles from moving inward or from "walking in the wind." McClintock describes the use of the liner in the summer and winter:

> The wall lining was also a protection from the hot sun in summer and helped keep out the heavy rains of spring and autumn. In warm weather we sometimes raised the lower part of the lodge cover from the ground for the wind to blow through; but in winter any open spaces around the bottom were chinked with grass and sod to keep out the cold.[18]

Many Sioux liner tops were decorated with porcupine quill-wrapped dangles having buffalo dew claws. When the wind shook the poles, the dangles gently chimed, and these were thought to attract the buffalo.

Many ozans had painted panel sections. Usually each painted panel had four triangular designs since four was a sacred number. A painted ozan brightened up a lodge and made the interior appear larger. Society tipis had liners with the drawn war exploits of their members depicting coups counted upon enemies. Clark Wissler, who worked for the American Museum of Natural History, describes the hanging of the liner:

> In a few tipis one may yet see a single or double back wall of soft dressed cow skins. When a pair of such back walls is used, they usually meet in the space between the backrests, though as may be expected, there is a great deal of variation in their adjustment. They are supported by a thong or rope tied to the successive poles, strings for this purpose being inserted at regular intervals along the up-

per edge of the back wall. While these are often rendered highly decorative, they are really practical. They serve to keep out the wind and any water that may find its way down the poles from their tops. They protect the people from draughts, as air can enter under the edge of the tipi, pass upward between the cover and the back wall and out over their heads, affording ventilation of the most approved type. There are five specimens in the collection, one of them of buffalo skins, about ten to twelve feet long and six feet wide. They are made of two skins, with a triangular piece extending upward between them to give the whole the proper shape to fit the surface of the conical interior. [19]

This painted Blackfoot liner was used to encircle half of a tipi.

A Lakota hide liner was often decorated with porcupine-quilled dangles. This painted liner is held back at its base with rocks.

UNIQUE TIPIS

One old photograph showed three Ute tipis which took advantage of a tree's stability. Each tipi had its own tree with lodgepoles placed into the high branches. The lodge cover overlapped the poles, except where allowance was made for branches to protrude through the front of the tipi cover.

This is Red Cloud's camp near Pine Ridge. In the foreground a tree appears to be used as a support for a tipi. (SDSHS)

Another example of a variation from the typical tipi is the oldest known Sioux tipi. It was made about 1770. This tipi was captured by the French around 1823. Later a French nobleman used it as a wall hanging before it was purchased by a German museum in 1846. Paintings on the cover record the legend of the sacred pipe, an important element to the Lakota culture. Because the ear flap pockets are on the opposite side of the drawings, we know the pictures were meant to be viewed while inside the tipi. This small Lakota tipi is described as follows:

> The height of the peak of the tipi measured 1.70 meters (5 feet 7 inches), and the diameter at the base was 2.45 meters (8 feet), which was smaller than those used for dwelling purposes. Some one hundred figures were drawn or painted on the inside of the cover. We know from Buffalo Hump that the tipi was erected with the figures on the inside.[14]

Warriors traveling into enemy country often made quick shelters from dead trees. This shelter is one of a half dozen that remain today.

These Ute families have placed their poles into trees and have incorporated much of the trees into their tipis. (Denver Public Library Western History Collection, Z186)

Another type of tipi was the large council tent. Here a large center pole was set firmly into the ground. Then lodgepoles were laid onto this main pole, and hide covers from two lodges were pinned together and placed around the framework to create a large half circle. This ingenious arrangement provided a shade for a large number of Lakota as described as here:

> Little Wound, one of the most powerful of Sioux chieftains, summoned the other leaders of his nation to his grand "council tepees," there to talk over a lasting peace and agency reforms. Two immense tepees were placed side by side and made to furnish room for one hundred men. [15]

Another tipi was the temporary structure set up by war parties. These groups traveled on foot, so they did not transport their regular lodges with them. While on a scouting expedition, the warriors would find lying dead trees to make a temporary framework to cover with hides tied together. Some brush shelters can still be found in remote areas.

In the earlier days when there were dog travois, a temporary tipi was sometimes constructed by stacking the travois and placing a hide tipi over the framework. Bird Woman describes the method:

> My husband, Son-of-a-Star, once told me of another way to make a tent out of dog travois. Three travois were joined together at their tops and a piece of tent skin drawn around the frame thus made. Two persons could be accommodated very well in such a shelter. [16]

The hide tipi existed as early as 1540 when Francisco Coronado reported seeing skin tents on his expedition through the Southwest. We know from the journals of Lewis and Clark that on April 7, 1805, a hide tipi was purchased for the captains to use as they departed on their 2000-mile journey to the Pacific Ocean. As the Corps of Discovery departed from their winter camp at Mandan, in present-day North Dakota, the group traveled by six canoes and two pirogues up the Missouri River. It is assumed that the cover and poles of Sacagawea's tipi were carried on one of the

Sitting Bull's council tent has a stout center pole supporting the poles of this large tipi cover. Usually several covers were pinned together to make a large shade. (SHSND C1427)

pirogues. Her tipi was large enough to accommodate five adults and one child. The tipi was used daily and eventually wore out. Charbonneau, Sacagawea's husband, was paid $500.33 for his this leather lodge, one horse and his services as a translator.

What is unique is the description of ties along the front of the tipi. I believe that early tipis possibly used leather thongs to close the front before the use of lacing pins. Meriwether Lewis describes the tipi's construction as follows:

> Captain Clark, myself, the two interpreters (Drouillard and Charbonneau), and the woman (Sacagawea) and child (Pomp) sleep in a tent of dressed hides. This tent is in the Indian style, formed of a number of dressed buffalo skins sewn together with sinews. It is cut in such [a] manner that when folded double, it forms the quarter of a circle and is left open at one side. Here it may be attached or loosened at pleasure by strings which are sewn to its sides for that purpose. [17]

Following the Civil War, muslin began to become somewhat available for tipi construction. It was a unique departure from the tanned buffalo hides. After the Battle of the Little Bighorn, most Native

Two travois are propped against each other (one at the right and one nearest the tipi). A third travois lies sideways against the other two. All have drying meat on their poles and platform hoops. (SDSHS)

Americans were not allowed to leave the reservation, and by 1890 the free-ranging bison were gone. A few Lakota still wanted a hide tipi, so they used steer hides for their lodges. Changes in tipi style slowly evolved, so the canvas tipi of today is somewhat different from the original hide tipi. The early reservation years saw ropes added for the first time to the bottom of the smoke flaps. These ropes ran to a pole in front of the tipi. This pulled the ear flaps outward to present a picturesque look to the front of the tipi. The cut-out doorway also came into vogue. This permitted an easier entrance into the lodge but added the problem of covering the large opening. Each hide tipi had half a buffalo tail intact as ornamentation at the tips of the smoke flaps. The canvas tipi owners now added buffalo beards above their smoke flap pockets as a remembrance of the hide tipis. Slits along the base of hide tipis for pegging the tipi to the ground were now substituted with peg loops or tied stones. Inside the tipi the liner or ozan had thongs placed near the bottom to tie to each tipi pole. The hide liners omitted this time-consuming duty by relying on the contents of the lodge and rocks to hold back the ozan. The most dramatic change was the look of the cover itself. The canvas did not display the interesting puzzle-like pattern of the sewn hides or allow those inside to view the glow of sunlight illuminating objects beyond the tipi.

Hide tipis often became dark at the top from the fires. The creosote from the smoke was beneficial for the hides; it coated the fibers to make them resistant to moisture.

LIVING IN A HIDE TIPI

A hide tipi is a practical year-round home. Among the Omaha Indians, it is reported that unlike other earth lodge tribes, they spent their winters in tipis and their summers in earth lodges. This was because the tipi was easier to heat in the winter due to its smaller area. On a night when it was zero degrees Fahrenheit outside, I recorded that the inside of a hide tipi with a fire and full liner was 50 degrees. If a hide ceiling (tiozan) were added to a tipi, the temperature might increase to 65 degrees with the same fire.

A buffalo hide tipi during the day is translucent with a warm, yellow-brown glow. The buffalo tails and quillwork decorations on the exterior appear as though they are part of the interior. The sewn hides also present an intriguing, puzzle-like pattern. The tipi poles spiral above the tipi cover to point to the sky in a pattern that the Lakota call "a nest." At night with a campfire, all the activity inside the tipi is clearly lit for the camp to see. It is like living in a lampshade, so for privacy a liner was often used. This also kept enemies from easily shooting an arrow at a silhouetted figure, as recorded on one winter count calendar. The areas of the tipi's interior are explained as follows:

A buffalo hide tipi is translucent so outside objects such as these smoke poles, tails and dangles are visible from inside the lodge.

> The inside of the tipi is a circular cone-shaped cavity...The fire is near the centre, though usually nearer the door than the rear, because the smoke hole is in front of the crossing of the poles. Sometimes the sides of the tipi are steeper in the rear and more sloping toward the front, thereby bringing the smoke hole near the centre. The fireplace is a small circle of water-worn stones. Just back of the fire, about halfway to the rear of the tipi is a small cleared space upon which sweet grass or other incense is burned from time to time as the ceremonial obligations of the family may require. This "smudge place" may be regarded as the family altar. At the sides toward the rear are the couches or beds. At the head of each couch is a wooden tripod supporting a back-rest made of willows strung with sinew. The beds are several thicknesses of old blankets laid on the ground, or upon a thin layer of hay. Pillows are used and the sleepers covered with blankets or quilts.[30]

Since the tipi was the property of the wife, she kept everything she had made if there was ever a divorce. She would announce the separation by placing her husband's articles outside the doorway. This would be everything except the man's weapons and religious items.

In moving camp the wife had the job of taking down the lodge and erecting it in the new location. The methods of folding a tipi are explained:

> Some women preferred to begin by rolling the sides of the lodge toward the center, then

This is the back of the tipi showing quilled tipi bags hanging on the inside. The outline of a tail, smoke poles and quilled decorations on the outside show through the buffalo skins.

LIVING IN A HIDE TIPI 63

At the rear of this tipi, the pattern of sewn hides can be seen above the tipi furnishings.

64 LIVING IN A HIDE TIPI

A hand-tanned buffalo hide is translucent, allowing the silhouette of a person to be visible through the tipi. A liner curtain offered privacy from shadows created by a campfire at night.

folded over the ear flaps, folding up a portion of the bottom and providing a somewhat larger pack. Others first made a fold along the vertical axis at the center and continued to fold the skin on this axis until the package was the width of the saddle, then folded or rolled up the top and bottom ends. [31]

It took less than an hour to "strike" a tipi and load belongings. Most families needed three or four horses in order to move their camp. One horse packed the tipi and liner. Two horses carried the poles, about five or six poles per side. These poles had burned holes through which they were laced. This kept individual poles from sliding out of the bundle. The last horse was for the wife to ride with household furnishings lashed onto a travois platform of two tipi poles. Her saddle usually had a rawhide breast collar and crupper. These kept the saddle from sliding back while she was traveling up a hill or forward when going downhill. A woman's saddle had high forks. This allowed the tipi liner to be placed in the seat of the saddle and allowed her to sit astride the bundle.

This is an upward view of converging tipi poles at the smoke opening.

This travois is transporting tipi poles and a child. In the background a man is smoking a peace pipe near the frame of a sweat lodge. (SDSHS)

A travois, consisting of poles lashed to a platform, was used to carry tipi furnishings. (SHSND 0739-v1-p52a)

This tipi's dangles and rosettes display the handiwork of women; painted horses with riders on the tipi cover show the artistry of men. (SDSHS)

CHILDREN

Children in the tipi could play but were taught to be quiet while doing so. For a small camp, maintaining quiet was important. Enemies were always a threat, so a child's noise invited a camp to be noticed. I have been told that long ago, as soon as a baby was born and cared for, it seldom cried. Whenever the baby screamed or bawled, the mother would gently pinch the nose and cover the mouth. The baby, unable to inhale, would stop crying to breathe, whereupon the mother released her hold. The next time the infant cried, the mother again held the nose and mouth shut. Because this was immediately done, the infant associated crying with suffocation. Even in a baby, crying showed a lack of courage.

In the tipi the children learned to give respect to elders. They refrained from speaking unless asked to speak. About age seven, a boy would no longer speak to his mother except through a third person. This practice was to keep a mother from destroying a boy's courage by keeping him from dangerous activities. Being coddled he would not be-

A play tipi belonging to the girl in the doorway is seen at the lower left corner. (SDSHS, USZ62-22970)

come brave—the most admired value to the Lakota. At about the age of seven, a boy was considered a man and would more often sit on the men's side of the lodge. He would not speak directly to his sister, to avoid incest. Because this avoidance was very awkward, the boy spent much of his time in a relative's tipi. In the Hunka Ceremony, he would likely be honored by being "adopted" by another person. He would be treated royally as a special member of this family.

Girls were given a small play tipi with which they could learn how to set up a full-sized lodge. The foot bones in the buffalo hoof were their play horses. These bone horses were colored by being dropped into porcupine quill dye baths.

This toy tipi has an added buckskin doll and buffalo foot bone horses.

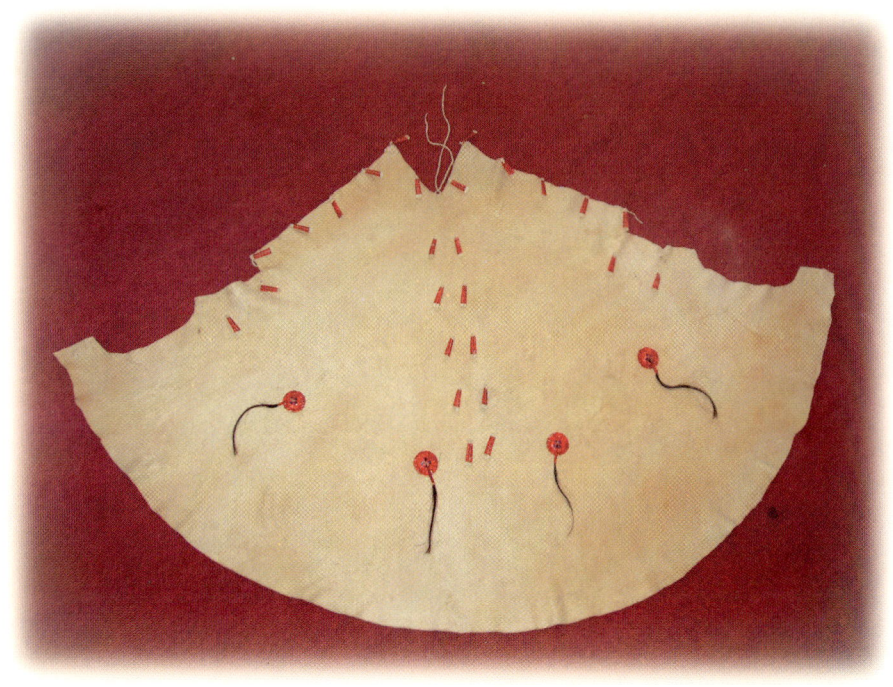

This child's tipi is a miniature copy of an adult lodge, but is less than a half circle.

WOMANHOOD

A girl about age seven was taught to be a woman. She was hereafter watched by an aunt or grandmother anytime she left the camp. This was to keep her safe from enemies that were always watching a village. She would not be allowed to play at will in the tipi but would sit on the women's side. Each girl would then be given a small chastity belt and taught to use it. She would be taught how to sew, prepare foods and tan hides. At puberty, she would go through a womanhood ceremony and usually marry a year or two later.

Several days each month a woman was not allowed to stay in her tipi. During her "moon," she stayed in a separate tipi near the outskirts of a village. The explanation is given as follows:

> At puberty a girl was secluded for four nights in a small tipi under the guardianship of an old woman. A married woman also had to withdraw while menstruating, as did the unmarried daughter of the owner of sacred objects, which otherwise were supposed to become polluted. [29]

TIPI ETIQUETTE

All tribes had rules on how to conduct themselves within a tipi. To enter a tipi, one had to be invited to come inside. If the cover flap was tossed to the side, anyone was permitted to enter and even to eat food from the fireplace. The Sioux said, "The chief's door should always be open." Generosity was one of the most important Lakota values.

If the door cover was in place, then a visitor gazed upward to see if the ear flaps were closed or open. If the occupants were gone, flaps were closed as they would be in a storm. If the smoke flaps were open, the occupants were inside and the visitor needed to let his presence be known. He could cough near the doorway, scratch on the cover or shake the buffalo hoof rattle used by some tipi owners. If those inside chose not to host a visitor, they simply ignored the request to enter.

If a visitor was invited into a lodge, he or she needed to first master a giant step above the entrance. In summer camp the pins below the entrance were often removed to ease this task. After the first foot en-

When a Lakota tipi entrance was open, anyone was permitted to walk into the lodge and help themselves to food. (SHSND 0087-099)

tered the tipi, a guest needed to duck low through the opening while also placing the other foot inside. On hide tipis there commonly were bison tails on opposite sides of the entrance. These provided convenient handholds to avoid tripping while entering the tipi.

There was a women's or a men's side to observe, and different tiyospaye (groups) of the Lakota practiced various rules at different times. Ultimately, it was the wife, as owner of the tipi, who set the rules. The practice that I found most universal was that the area to the left (upon entering the lodge) was the female side with the right being the male side. This reasoning was based upon the consideration that the

RATTLE
Some families had buffalo hoof rattles attached to the right of the door. These were shaken by someone requesting permission to enter the tipi.

The smoke flaps were closed to prevent snow from entering this tipi.

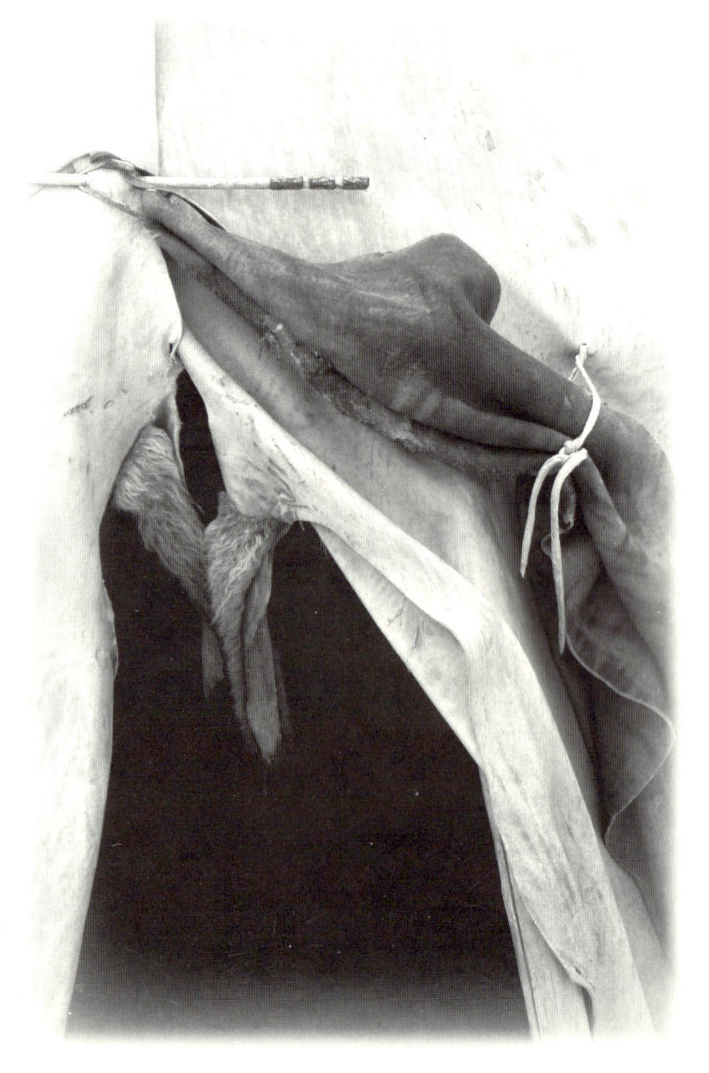

The buffalo tails at the doorway were grasped to steady those entering the tipi. When the tails were tied, it was a signal to not enter the tipi.

sun of the south is warming and nurturing (with the tipi facing the east) so this area is identified as feminine. The north side is the direction associated with winter's challenges demanding fortitude, so this was the masculine side. Stephen R. Riggs worked in the mid-1800's translating the Bible into the Dakota language. He reported on the designated areas he observed as he visited inside Dakota tipis:

> The wife's place is on the left side as one enters, the right side as one sits in the back part. The children come in between the mother and father. The place of the grandmother or mother-in-law or aunt is the corner by the door opposite the woman of the house. If a man has more wives than one, they have separate tipis or arrange to occupy the different sides of one. [20]

James R. Walker stayed from 1896 until 1914 on the Pine Ridge Reservation. In his book *Lakota Societies*, Walker reverses the gender sides.

> The place in the tipi opposite the door is the catku. This belongs to the man. He sits and sleeps here. The fireplace is in the center of the lodge. The woman sits at right of it looking from the door, or at the left of the man. If there are two women, then the favorite of the man sits at this place and the other on the opposite side of the fire, or if they are sisters they may sit side by side. The oldest son sits with the father on the catku until he is about six years old. One is honored in the tipi by being asked to sit on the catku. [21]

Opposite the doorway was the reserved area for the husband, called "catku" by the Sioux. The painted buffalo robe of the husband was often hung near his willow backrest.

William Powers, author of *Oglala Religion*, agreed with Walker regarding gender sides. His interpretation is based upon an interpretation of the cosmos and its connection with the cardinal directions:

> ...[in] the floor plan of an Oglala tipi... we see that the catku, or place of honor, is located at the west; the women's side is at the north, or on the left (from the perspective of the catku); the tiyopa, or doorway, is at the east; the men's side is at the south, or right (again viewed from the catku). [22]

My interviews with the elders clarify the varying interpretations involving gender sides between the Oglala and most Sioux groups. I was told by one Oglala elder that prior to the reservation, they observed the left side, upon entering, as the female side. After the reservation, the gender sides for some Oglala were reversed, but no one could explain their reasoning behind the change.

The Sioux had an appropriate direction to walk while inside a tipi. Because the fireplace, anchor pegs, and altar were in the middle of the tipi, travel needed to be either to the right or left. Most agree that in a large gathering of men in a council tent, the host leds the group by traveling to his left, and the group followed until the entire circle of the lodge was filled. In this situation practicality took over and the women honored the men by giving up their area. This was the rule in the sweat lodge and also in the large council tent. At other times the male or female guests went directly to their appropriate sides without following a full circle. Many of the Sioux groups would agree with Reginald Laubin, author of *The Indian Tipi*, that in general practice, visiting men entered to their right (or to the left for the Oglala of today) and proceeded to where they were directed by the host. The altar in the back was not crossed. The book *The Indians* echoes this rule:

> When a male visitor enters the tipi he goes to the right and waits for the host to invite him to sit in the guest place to the left of the owner at the rear. A woman enters after the man and goes to the left. [23]

If a meal was part of the visit, guests were expected to bring their buffalo horn spoons and bowls from which they would eat. The Sioux rules for eating are described as follows:

> At a feast, the men were served first, and in an all-male gathering, as a warrior-society meeting or a religious ritual, the younger men were appointed to act as servants. The host waited until his guests had been served and had eaten before partaking of the food himself...The guests were expected to eat everything put before them or to invite others to eat it, or to carry it home with them. They offended the host if they refused anything offered to them. [24]

An important meeting might have a "smoke." If the host of the lodge had a Catlinite peace pipe, it was often housed in a pipe bag placed on a moose pan altar behind the fire circle. The pipe bowl and stem were connected while still inside the bag and the bowl filled with red willow bark tobacco. After the pipe was lit, it was smoked by each person while being passed in a sunwise (clockwise) circle and then rested during the meeting on the tines of the antler moose pan. Later, when the pipe was picked up to

UTENSILS
It was expected that visitors bring their own bowl, buffalo horn cup and spoon when invited to a meal.

be cleaned of its ashes, it was a signal for the guests to leave the tipi.

Samuel Pond was active among the Dakota in the 1840's and worked on the translation of the Bible into their language. He spent much of his translating time within the tipis of the Eastern Sioux that he visited and explained their code of conduct:

> The side of the tent opposite the door was considered the place of honor. The owner of the tent and his wife usually occupied one side. The woman sat nearest the door, for the purpose of being near the cooking utensils, and for convenience in reaching the wood, which lay just outside the door. Lady visitors did not pass by the men, but sat down between them and the door, though no space in the tent was interdicted to women; and when men were not in the way, they sat where they pleased. I have many times seen those who were engaged in needlework occupying the place opposite the door, while men were in the house. The tent belonged not to the man but to the woman, and she occupied that part of it which was the most convenient for the

TIPI SIDES

- Catku with willow backs (seat for guest-of-honor)
- West
- Crossed anchor pegs to hold down the tipi
- South
- Woman's Side
- Man's Side
- North
- Altar
- Storage
- Storage
- Fireplace
- Doorway
- East

The gender sides are reversed by some Lakota groups

work she had to do… None were permitted to stand upright in the tent when it could be avoided.[25]

In the tipi, women did not sit cross-legged, as men, but with their legs tucked to one side or the other. The other posture, principally while doing quillwork, was to sit with legs extended so their project could be on their laps. It is surprising that without tables and chairs, women could execute intricate bead and quillwork.

Mrs. Red Warbonnet said that her grandmother served the men from near the entrance during social events. As they left, her grandmother would spin herself halfway around with her back to the fire and cover her head as the men filed out of her tipi.

The Cheyenne usually were friends with the Lakota and were often intermarried with Lakota. They practiced similar rules of etiquette as follows:

The place of honor is opposite the door. It is least subject to drafts, and no one need pass between that place and the fire. Here is the couch of the head of the family, unless guests are installed there, when he sleeps on the south side. Weapons and medicine bundles usually hang at the head of his bed. Saddlery lies next to the door on the south, as the woman's utensils on the north. Water hangs in a bucket (formerly a paunch) from one of the poles out of reach of the dogs. Wood is piled just south of the door outside.[26]

When there were several wives, the favorite one slept beside the husband. This was usually in the guest area, or catku, since there was more headroom there. Exceptions were made when needed as sleeping areas were changed to accommodate the number of people. Of utmost importance was accessibility to the warmth of the fire in the wintertime.

Most camps were pitched in a circle. Men used the central area to conduct their business while women worked in the solitude of a shaded place away from the men. (SDSHS)

In the early days, the village was set up with the tipis pitched close together in a large open-ended circle. The center area was for games, visiting and social activities. The men usually had to themselves this area where they visited, worked on their weapons and guarded their horses tethered near the entryway. The space behind the tipis was where the women conducted their visiting and engaged in craftwork. It was here the women could avoid interaction with men. Luther Standing Bear explains how a mother-in-law and son-in-law needed to avoid interaction:

But whenever father was at home and he chanced to walk out of the tipi, he covered his face with his blanket until he was sure that he would not see his mother-in-law. In this way he showed his respect for her, and had he not observed this courtesy she would have had every right to be affronted. She, too, avoided him, and if by chance they met, she hid her face. Had she allowed him to look upon her, it would have been an unforgivable breach of manners. 27

EXITING THE TIPI

While in the tipi, it was rude to pass in front of another guest. Such movement blocked the light from the fire and gave momentary shadows to others. In a large council tipi, a person could walk behind others as they bent forward. However, in the average tipi, there was no headroom to walk behind guests, so someone leaving needed to walk in front of others and beg to be excused. Therefore, once an occasion began, all were expected to stay. If an individual needed to go to the restroom, he would not be so crude as to tell everyone that he was going to relieve himself. He would simply say, "I am going to check on my horses!"

WINKTES

In some villages, there were men who were afraid of warfare or male activities. Such a person was called a "winkte." He often wore a dress with quill or beaded strips to show he was a man. This person was avoided by other men but was not looked down upon. He was thought to have unique powers. Warriors would go into a winkte's tipi to determine how they would fare in an upcoming battle. The winkte were said to see into the future. It was said that a winkte was "wakan" or holy. Luther Standing Bear explains the role of winktes:

Everyone accepted the winktes with kindness and allowed them to choose their own work, be it either man's or woman's, and one of the bravest men I ever knew was a winkte. They were scarce, however, and in my life I have not known more than half a dozen. 28

THE CROSSING OF STREAMS

Many of the streams or rivers of the Great Plains are narrow. At times, such as during heavy rains, they can become swollen and difficult to cross. The sedentary tribes, such as the Mandan and Hidatsa, had bull boats to cross rivers. In migratory Plains tribes, the tipi cover became a temporary boat as told here:

…lodge covers were rolled up at the sides, baggage and children placed in them, and the women swam along behind pushing the

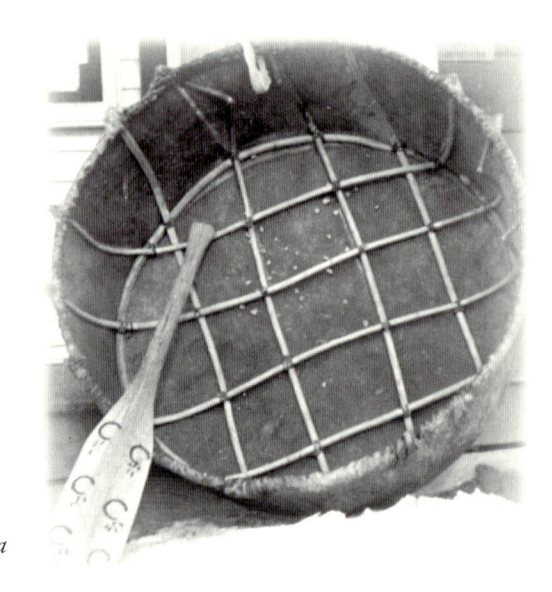

A buffalo hide has been shaped over a willow framework. (SHSND 0779-p22g)

Owl Woman and Many Grows are bending willows to form the framework of a bullboat. This type of boat was used by Plains tribes. (SHSND 0086-1108)

covers while men towed them from in front by ropes. The lodgepoles were placed under the travois and bound to them to form

crude rafts on which backrests and other luggage were transported over the water. Horses towed these improvised rafts.[32]

A woman is paddling a bullboat across the Missouri River. (SHSND 0086-1113)

DISCARDING OF OLD TIPI COVERS

The elderly and needy among the Lakota received a lodge secondhand when another family replaced their hide cover:

> …poor families often were content to rely upon the kindness of wealthy men to give them old lodge covers after they had made new ones. The rich family's large cover was cut down to meet the needs by trimming several feet off the base of it to make a much smaller conical. [33]

A folded tent provided a convenient seat for working behind the tipi. When the camp moved, it served as a rainproof cover for the furnishings:

> All of the items placed on a travois sometimes were wrapped in an old lodge cover and tied securely with rawhide rope 2 to 3 fingers wide, to protect them from dust, rain, or snow. [34]

The bottom of this hide tipi has rotted. Such a tipi was frequently donated to a poor family who would cut off the damaged section and use the top for their lodge. One of the buffalo hides sewn into this tipi cover is visible along the lower half of this lodge. (A pole extending through the smoke flap shows this to be an Arapaho tipi.) (SHSND A0369)

INTERVIEW WITH MRS. RED WARBONNET REGARDING TIPIS

While living among the Oglala Sioux, I was fortunate to know an elderly Lakota woman who had lived with her two grandmothers in a hide tipi. The following are interviews compiled from several sessions with her. She granted permission to use the conversations that I recorded and requested me to use her Hunka name rather than her married name. She has been gone for many years, but her candid comments give a capsule look into the days when hide tipis provided everything necessary for the glory days of the Lakota Nation.

Q. While living on the Pine Ridge Sioux Reservation, I met many old Lakota, but few lived in tipis; they lived in wall tents. How did you come to live in a tipi?

A. I lived with two grandmothers from the age of three until fifteen. The grandmothers were with Sitting Bull's band. But when the chief was killed, they left to join Big Foot's band who were escaping from the Cheyenne River Sioux Reservation to meet with Red Cloud on the Pine Ridge Reservation. This

The picture shows Sitting Bull's winter camp with doorways secured against wind and snow. (SHSND C0313-1)

group was soon involved in the Wounded Knee Massacre. One grandmother caught a horse and rode double with her daughter to escape during this battle. The other was a Woman Warrior and joined with warriors at the Stronghold. Later the sisters found each other and lived near Grass Creek. Both had tipis because they were traditional women. Neither had a surviving husband. I had been sick for 18 months, so they decided to care for me and teach me the old ways.

Q. Why didn't your parents raise you?

A. When I was about two, there was a celebration near a river. I was walking along the bank, and my cousin pushed me over the edge. I fell on top of many gopher hills. The gophers were mad, and they cast a spell on me. With their curse, I swelled up. My skin got so tight that it started to rip. I was taken to a hospital where I stayed 18 months. When I got better, there was a celebration at my parents' place for my return. At the meal, my grandmother spoke up. She told my dad that she wanted to take me as "one brought back from death." My father agreed. I do not know why, but my mother said nothing. I lived with my grandmothers until they both died when I was 15.

Q. What do you remember about your tipi?

A. I lived with one grandmother, and the other had her tipi next to ours. At night I slept with my grandmother in the guest-of-honor area, called "catku" in Lakota. At night we rolled up the backrests that were there. We had three or four inches of a dried reddish grass under my bed. I think you call it "little bluestem." My grandmother and I would gather this to cover the ground inside the tipi. It was a good insulation. We also put this grass in our moccasins in the wintertime to keep our feet warm. On the dried grass, we would have a buffalo hide base and on top we would have elk skin covers.

In our tipi we had three backrests. Two were for the guests-of-honor. If there were no guests, then I usually sat on one and my grandmother on another. In the summer with the front of the tipi opened up, I could watch outside what was happening. We sat on the bottom of the willow rests and leaned against the slanted upper part.

Our tipi faced east most of the year. We liked the morning sun to awaken us. Part of the year we moved our tipi to have the prevailing wind to hit the back of the tipi. The wind pushing against the back of the lodge forced the smoke out of the tipi. Most of the year, the wind comes from the west, so our tipi faced the opposite direction, or east. In some seasons, we faced southeast or southwest, depending on where most of the winds struck the back of the lodge.

Q. Did you ever have a problem keeping your tipi up in strong winds?

A. My grandmothers always made sure that the tripod of the tipi did not move. If any of the three main poles moved, everything would also move because the framework rests on the tripod. When the tipi was set up, we used a hatchet and hit the ground next to each pole. The hatchet head would be moved sideways, and the pole slid into the opening. We also tied the anchor rope to a y-shaped stake in the tipi when a storm was coming; otherwise the rope was loosely wrapped around the north tripod pole to be out of the way and not staked down. If we had a long camp—but always in winter—we put very large, heavy rocks in front of every pole. We made sure the rocks were flat so the poles could not slide the stones. With a circle of rocks in front of the poles and the tipi tied down, the tipi would not move. Above the tipi stakes, we often laid logs to keep the cover down.

Q. How did you keep warm in the winter?

A. Most of the year we had an ozan curtain made of hides. Our tipi had three sections that we could tie up. These ozans were tied to a hide rope that started at the door and wound around every other pole. During the summer, we only put up one section of liner in the back. In the winter, the ozan curtain touched the ground and had about a foot of hide tucked inside the entire tipi. We often used the heavy, flat rocks that had earlier been used in front of the tipi poles and put these rocks on the liner base. This kept the poles from moving, as before, but it also kept the liner at a slant; otherwise the liner would drape straight down. Rocks or our tipi furnishings kept the wind from blowing underneath the ozan.

Q. How did you survive when it got very cold?

A. When it got below zero for a long time, we would put a rope across the back of the tipi tied from side to side at the guest-of-honor area. The rope would be just high enough so my grandmother could walk under it. The hides would make a low roof that would slant slightly toward the rear of the tipi and reach the top of the liner. This was like a low ceiling. The Lakota name for this was "tiozan." We also would add two more ropes to have a tiozan on each side of the doorway going toward the back. This was also covered with

At night the willow backrests were turned to face each other. This became a sleeping area when pillows and hides were added.

hides placed over the ropes and tucked along where the liner rope ran. When the three tiozans were in place, there was only a small opening for the smoke of the fireplace near the entrance.

Q. How was your fireplace constructed?

A. The grass and dirt were dug out of a circle area forward of the anchor rope. The removed dirt was placed in the back of the fireplace and trampled to slope toward the catku area. The pit was shallow in front and deeper in the back. The sloping pit, we thought, threw more heat to the back and the coals would roll downhill between the logs to keep us warmer. In the hole, two logs were placed headed east and west. The fire was made by striking two flint-like rocks together above a bunch of dried reddish grass. We would catch the spark and blow on the grass to get a fire made. Small sticks were used between the logs to get larger sticks or dried chips to burn. The fire was only fed new fuel from the front side, near the door. Sometimes we had rocks near the fire and at night we would wrap these hot stones to be placed near our feet to keep them warm.

Q. Did your tipi have decorations on the outside?

A. My one grandmother had been a woman warrior. She tied a whip below the tail at the top of the lifting pole. This was a great honor for all to see.

My other grandmother had tied to the top of her lifting pole two rabbit ears along with a fluff of the rabbit's tail. This showed she was looking for a husband. The Lakota men would tease each other and say, "Watch out, she's a man getter!"

The long tail ornament on the lifting pole, painted tails on the cover and a staff by the door indicates this tipi belonged to an important leader. (SHSND 0198-09)

Q. What did you do when it was going to rain?

A. We would bring the ear flap poles from the back of the tipi to the front, overlapping one tipi flap on the other. My grandmothers also had hides sewn together that had some pockets in the corners. They would lift this hide canopy and place it over the tips of the tipi poles. In those days we had short poles. It would also overlap part of the tipi cover and keep rain from coming down the poles.

Q. What did you have for meals during the day?

A. We had no special times to eat as you do today. Whenever anyone was hungry, we could always reach into a bladder bag hanging on the women's side of my grandmother's tipi. Inside was what you call "pemmican," but we call it "wasna." This was pounded up dried meat and chokecherries with a little suet added. This kept indefinitely because it was a dry powder. Just a little was enough to keep a person filled for a long time.

In the morning we just had a tea. It was made of spearmint or peppermint leaves that we gathered near the creek. For a special treat, we sometimes had pieces of meat cooked in a paunch or stomach. For this, my grandmother put four poles into the ground to hold the stomach which was filled with water. To heat the water, we added hot rocks using y-shaped sticks. After a half dozen rocks were added, the water would start to boil. It took about an hour to cook the soup. Usually we added tinpsila (prairie turnips) to flavor the soup.

Q. What training did you receive as you were growing up?

A. When I was eight, I was given a small buckskin belt. It wrapped between my legs and had buckskin strings to tie at my side. I was told what to do as a woman. Everywhere I went, if very far, one of my grandmothers would go with me.

At about 12 years old, I had my womanhood ceremony. My hair was parted and red ochre put on the part line. I had a blue dot put on my forehead. This was so Tunkasila (Grandfather) would know us if we passed out of this life. I was given a new name. I was given a wider chastity belt, and womanhood duties were told to me. I was told how to go to the woman's tipi. When I would be able to tan a hide and make my first pair of moccasins, I would be eligible for marriage and could hang an awl, knife and strike-a-light cases from my beaded belt.

Q. Please tell me how the woman's lodge was used.

A. Once a month, usually for four days, a woman could not be in her own tipi. To be there would be "too powerful" for the medicine things and might cause harm to the men. There was a special tipi set up away from camp that all the women would use. Inside, a large pile of sage was stacked up, and the woman would sit on the mound of sage. Each day new sage would be brought and the old sage burned. A grandmother or relative would be caring for the person with food. After four days, the woman would be purified in a sweat lodge.

Q. When I give seminars, one of the asked questions is "How did they go to the restroom while living in a village?"

A. When a girl or woman had to relieve herself, she would always go with an escort. There were always enemies around so we had to be careful. The women went away from camp; women used one direction and men another.

The women had long dresses so they could kneel, lean back and relieve themselves with no one seeing because such dresses reached to the ground.

Q. How could you ride horses with such long dresses?

A. An early buckskin dress had panels on each side of the dress. These were longer than the front and back of the dress. The two tabs on each side of the dress could be tied around each leg. The dresses were loose so that a woman could sit on the horse and not have her legs be seen. Leggings also in the early days came much higher than are worn today.

Q. What do you know about dating?

A. The best place to meet girls was as they came daily to draw water. Boys would flirt, but the girls were escorted so there was little time to talk. If a boy was interested in courting a girl, he would whisper, "I'll see you tonight." Such a boy would come to the girl's tipi in the evening with a robe over his head to hide who he was. In case of rejection, he would not be embarrassed. The girl would peek from out of the tipi opening to see if the boy was coming. When the boy arrived, the girl moved the doorway cover aside and stood. The boy's robe would be wrapped around the couple to give them privacy. The robe muffled any conversation from those listening inside the lodge. The parents knew the girl was safe because, although her upper body was outside the tipi, her lower half was inside the lodge and her moccasins could always be seen. At any time that the girl disliked what was happening, she ducked inside the tipi, leaving an embarrassed boy standing outside and alone.

Q. How did families arrange a marriage?

A. When a boy and girl were serious about each other, the parents were consulted. The father of a girl always had the power to decide for his daughter. Before the boy could even date, he had to have a feather. An eagle feather was earned for an enemy touched or killed in battle. Without a feather earned, the boy had not proven his bravery or manhood.

Usually the girls married a year or two after their womanhood ceremony and after they had been taught tanning skills. Boys were commonly 18, 21 or much older. The prospective suitor had to have prize horses to offer as a bride price. It took time to steal enemy horses necessary to honor a popular girl. Once the boy had a sufficient number of horses, they were brought to the parents' tipi. If the girl took the horses to water, the offer of marriage was accepted. The girl's family would return an equal number of horses to the boy's family to seal the marriage proposal.

Q. I know you are fluent in the Lakota language. Can you give me the names for the parts of the tipi?

A. I will start at the top. They are
   pole—tusu
   rope tie--wikan
   ear flap—wizipaha
   lacing pin—wiceska
   rosette—wakeyaskapi
   door—tiyopa
   peg—wihinpaspe
   bottom—wihuta

Q. One last question. What happened to the hide tipi and your grandmothers' things?

A. My grandmothers both died close to each other, less than a year apart. When my last grandmother died, I gave away everything. I wish now that someone had stopped me. I gave away the tipi, liners, buffalo hides—everything. When someone dies, the Lakota way is to honor the person by giving away everything and to have a large feed for the mourners. This generosity is a strong Lakota value.

Generosity was one of the most admired virtues of the Lakota. The tipis and handiwork on display will be given away after a large meal is served. (SHSND A1473)

IN RETROSPECT

Stanley Campbell, an early ethnologist, wrote a scientific paper about tipis. At the conclusion of his writing, he put aside his objectivity to express his feelings for the tipi:

It would be a thousand pities if this staunchest, handsomest, and most comfortable of tents should be lost to American civilization. [35]

There is a sense of dignity and pride on the faces of the Lakota group in the next photograph. The tipis were carefully constructed by the women and embellished with their finest porcupine quillwork. These proud people boldly showed their citizenship by raising the American flag on the honoring pole. I hope the reader has gained greater understanding and appreciation for the Buffalo Nation and its rich traditions surrounding the buffalo hide tipi.

(SDSHS)

This is Sitting Bull's camp from a time when the Sioux lived in tipis and freely roamed the Great Plains. *(SHSND 0022-H-0042)*

KEY:
   Photo Courtesy of the State Historical Society of North Dakota—State Archives is identified as "SHSND."
   Photo Courtesy of the South Dakota State Historical Society—State Archives is identified at "SDSHS."

END NOTES

1. David A. Dary, The Buffalo Book (Swallow Press, Ohio University Press, 1974), p. 113.

2. E. Douglas Branch, The Hunting of the Buffalo (University of Nebraska Press, 1962), p. 51.

3. James Mooney, "Smithsonian Anthropological," Field notes #2213.

4. Samuel W. Pond, The Dakota or Sioux in Minnesota as They Were in 1834 (Minnesota Historical Collections, Vol. 12, 1908), p. 38.

5. Gene Weltfish, The Lost Universe (Basic Book, Inc., New York, 1965), p. 144.

6. Clark Wissler, Societies and Ceremonial Associations in the Oglala Division of the Teton-Dakota, "Anthropological Papers of the American Museum of Natural History," Vol. XI, part 1 (New York, 1912), p. 79.

7. Gilbert L. Wilson, "Anthropological Papers of the American Museum of Natural History," Vol. XV, part II (American Museum Press, New York, 1924), p. 224.

8. Gilbert L. Wilson, "Anthropological Papers of the American Museum of Natural History," Vol. XV, part II (American Museum Press, New York, 1924), p. 143.

9. Stanley Campbell, "American Anthropologist" (N. S., 17, 1915), p. 686.

10. Clark Wissler, Societies and Ceremonial Associations in the Oglala Division of the Teton-Dakota, "Anthropological Papers of the American Museum of Natural History," Vol. XI, part l (New York, 1912), pp. 111-12.

11. Peter Nabokov and Robert Easton, Native American Architecture (Oxford University Press, Oxford, 1989), p. 163.

12. High Dog, "High Dog's Winter Count," North Dakota Historical Collections, Bismarck, North Dakota.

13. Samuel W. Pond, The Dakota or Sioux in Minnesota as They Were in 1834 (Minnesota Historical Collections, Vol. 12, 1908), p. 38.

14. "The Indian Trader," Vol. 8, No. 6, June, 1977.

15. Richard G. Hardorff, The Death of Crazy Horse (University of Nebraska Press, Lincoln, 1998), p. 47.

16. Gilbert L. Wilson, "Anthropological Papers of the American Museum of Natural History, " Vol. XV, part II (American Museum Press, New York, 1924), p. 143.

17. Ronald Turner, As Told: The Journals of Lewis and Clark (The Narrative Press, California, 2003), p. 102.

18. Walter McClintock, "Southwest Museum Leaflets," No. 5 (Southwest Museum, Los Angeles, California), p. 4.

19. Clark Wissler, "Anthropological Papers of the American Museum of Natural History," Vol. V, part l (New York, 1909), p. 106.

20. Stephen R. Riggs, "North American Ethnology," Vol. IX (Government Printing Office, Washington, 1893), p. 204.

21. James R. Walker, Lakota Society (University of Nebraska Press, 1982), p. 40.

22. William Powers, Oglala Religion (University of Nebraska Press, 1975), p. 176.

23. Benjamin Capps, The Indians (Time-Life, Inc., 1973), p. 91.

24. Reginald and Gladys Laubin, The Indian Tipi (University of Oklahoma Press, Norman, 1977), p. 113.

25. Samuel W. Pond, The Dakota or Sioux in Minnesota as They Were in 1834 (Minnesota Historical Collections, Vol. 12, 1908), pp. 38-39.

26. William K. Powers, Oglala Religion (University of Nebraska Press, 1975), pp. 176-77.

27. Stanley Campbell, "American Anthropologist" (N. S., 17, 1915), p. 686.

28. Luther Standing Bear, Land of the Spotted Eagle (University of Nebraska Press, 1933), p. 93.

29. Robert H. Lowie, Indians of the Plains (American Museum of Natural History, University of Nebraska Press, 1954), p. 84.

30. Clark Wissler, "Anthropological Papers of the American Museum of Natural History," Vol. V, part 1, (New York, 1912), p. 105.

31. John C. Ewers, The Horse in the Blackfoot Culture, Smithsonian Institution, Bureau of American Ethnology, Bulletin 159 (Smithsonian Institution Press, Washington, 1955), p. 133.

32. John C. Ewers, The Horse in the Blackfoot Culture, Smithsonian Institution, Bureau of American Ethnology, Bulletin 159 (Smithsonian Institution Press, Washington, 1955), p. 144.

33. John C. Ewers, The Horse in the Blackfoot Culture, Smithsonian Institution, Bureau of American   Ethnology, Bulletin 159 (Smithsonian Institution Press, Washington, 1955), p. 132.

34. John C. Ewers, The Horse in the Blackfoot Culture, Smithsonian Institution, Bureau of American Ethnology, Bulletin 159 (Smithsonian Institution Press, Washington, 1955), p. 135.

35. Stanley Campbell, "American Anthropologist, Vol. 17, No. 4, October-December, 1915 (The New Era Printing Company, Pennsylvania), p. 694.